FORMED IN CH

ABOUT THE SERIES

Who is Jesus Christ? What does it mean to know him? What do the Church and her sacraments have to do with him? How are we to follow him?

These are the questions at the heart of the Catholic faith, and these are the questions the Formed in Christ series answers. Rooted in the story of Salvation History and steeped in the writings of the Fathers and Doctors of the Church, this series of high school textbooks from the St. Paul Center seeks to engage minds and hearts as it presents the tenets of the Catholic faith in Scripture and Tradition.

Over the course of this comprehensive, four-year curriculum, students will learn the fundamentals of Church teaching on the Person and mission of Jesus Christ, Sacred Scripture, the Church, the sacraments, morality, Church history, vocations, Catholic social teaching, and more. Just as important, they'll be invited, again and again, to enter more deeply into a relationship with Christ, growing in love of him as they grow in knowledge of him.

PUBLISHED

Evidence of Things Unseen: An Introduction to Fundamental Theology
Andrew Willard Jones and Louis St. Hilaire.
Edited by Stimpson Chapman

The Word Became Flesh: An Introduction to Christology
Andrew Willard Jones. Edited by Emily Stimpson Chapman

That You Might Have Life: An Introduction to the Paschal Mystery of Christ
Louis St. Hilaire. Edited by Emily Stimpson Chapman

I Will Build My Church: An Introduction to Ecclesiology
Andrew Willard Jones. Edited by Emily Stimpson Chapman

Do This in Remembrance: An Introduction to the Sacraments
Jacob Wood. Edited by Emily Stimpson Chapman

Christ Alive in Us: An Introduction to Moral Theology
John Meinert and Emily Stimpson Chapman

THE WORD BECAME FLESH

AN INTRODUCTION TO CHRISTOLOGY

THE WORD BECAME FLESH

AN INTRODUCTION TO CHRISTOLOGY

ANDREW WILLARD JONES
Edited by Emily Stimpson Chapman

EMMAUS
ROAD
PUBLISHING

www.emmausroad.org
Steubenville, Ohio

In Grateful Recognition of Lawrence Joseph & Lynn Marie Blanford

Emmaus Road Publishing
1468 Parkview Circle
Steubenville, Ohio 43952

©2019 St. Paul Center
All rights reserved. Published 2019
Printed in the United States of America

Library of Congress Control Number: 2019934889

ISBN 978-1-949013-38-2

Cover image: *Virgin and Child in Clouds* (c. 1660), Bartolomé Esteban Murillo
Rijksmuseum, Amsterdam

Cover design and layout by Margaret Ryland

TABLE OF CONTENTS

Part I

God and Revelation

As a Christian, you are called to a personal relationship with God. Protestants tend to say this more often than Catholics, but Catholics believe this as well. Catholics believe that God has invited all of us to a close, intimate relationship with himself, and that he wants us to enter into that relationship now, while we live on earth, although the relationship won't be perfectly realized until heaven.

But how do you go about having a personal relationship with God? What does it even mean to have a personal relationship with God? What does that look like? The answer to those questions comes to us through the Person of Jesus Christ. In this course, you'll get to know God better, as Father, Son, and Holy Spirit. You'll learn about what faith really is, how you're called to live that faith in a community of believers, and how your relationship with God will prepare you for eternal life.

First, though, in Part I, we're going to look at how God has revealed himself to humanity, becoming a man himself as Jesus and inviting us to a relationship with him. We'll also look at faith, which is our acceptance of God's invitation. Through faith, we learn to know God. This knowledge, in turn, moves us to become disciples, which means we live out our faith in our daily lives. As you'll see, revelation, faith, and discipleship are all linked and come together definitively in the communion of the faithful that we call the Catholic Church.

Chapter 1

Revelation:
God's Gift of Himself

ASSIGNED READING
Psalm 19
John 1
Hebrews 1:1–4
CCC 76–82

Divine Revelation

From the beginning of history, God has repeatedly shown his love and desire for a relationship with us. As St. John exclaims, "We love because he first loved us" (1 John 4:19). Precisely because God loved us first, he has made himself known to us through his revelation.

In the Introduction to Fundamental Theology (Course 1), we explored the meaning of revelation, but it's a good idea to start this course on the Person of Jesus Christ—that is, the theological study called Christology—with a brief review. Revelation is God's communication of himself, and it comes to us in two different forms: natural and divine. Natural revelation is found in creation (CCC 32). Since God created the cosmos and everything in it, creation reveals information about God. Just as a painting reveals something about the artist who created it, nature—the created world—reveals something about the One who created it. Through nature, we can know that God exists, we can perceive his rationality, and we can begin to perceive his greatness. The splendor of a sunset, the vastness of the ocean, and the beauty of a rose all tell us something about who God is.

Natural revelation, however, is limited. We can know some things about God by looking at his creation, but that knowledge falls far short of the vast mystery that is God. God recognizes this, which is why revelation doesn't end with natural revelation. Because God wants to have a deeply personal relationship with us, his self-revelation goes beyond nature. This is called Divine Revelation. Through Divine Revelation, God intervenes directly in history, guiding his people toward a relationship with him that is salvific—that is, toward a relationship that saves us from our sin.

The story of God's revelation, of his interaction through both words and deeds with humanity, is called Salvation History. Salvation History started with Adam, continued through all the history of Israel, and culminated in the birth, life, death, and Resurrection of Jesus Christ. Jesus is the definitive act of Divine Revelation because Jesus was God himself entering history. Salvation History continues in the life of the Church, of which we are a part.

Scripture, Tradition, and the Deposit of Faith

God has revealed himself in history, through the patriarchs, the prophets, his angels, and definitively through his Son Jesus Christ. God's revelation of himself in time is the core of what we mean by Divine Revelation. But, Divine Revelation has another layer to it. God hasn't just intervened directly in history; he also has intervened in *our* communication of those historical events. What this means is that God has inspired humanity's actions and language so that we can accurately communicate the things God has said and done, making it possible for those who didn't witness these events to still know about them. This is called the Transmission of

Divine Revelation (CCC 74). The Transmission of Divine Revelation can be divided into two broad categories: Scripture and Tradition

> Scripture is the inspired written record of Salvation History. It consists of the Old Testament, which tells the story of Israel before the coming of Jesus, and the New Testament, which tells the story of Jesus and the early Church. When we say that the Scripture is inspired we mean that it has the Holy Spirit as its author. It is inerrant, meaning that everything in it is just as God wants it: Scripture has no "mistakes." (CCC 81)

In addition to Scripture, revelation is transmitted through the Church's Sacred Tradition. Tradition is a complicated concept. The Church doesn't believe that everything we need or ought to know about God is contained only in the Bible. Rather, she holds that Jesus taught his Apostles many things that weren't written down. The Bible itself tells us this. In 2 Thessalonians 2:15, St. Paul writes, "So then, brethren, stand firm and hold to the traditions which you were taught by us, either by word of mouth or by letter." In order to help the Church faithfully transmit Sacred Tradition, Jesus, after his Ascension into heaven, sent the Holy Spirit to guide the Apostles (John 14:26; Acts 2:1–4). Ever since, the Holy Spirit has continued to give this guidance to the Apostles' successors: the bishops. Likewise, the process of bishops replacing bishops, from the Apostles' time through today, is also guided by the Holy Spirit and is known as Apostolic Succession.

But, Tradition is not just an inspired version of the grade school game "Telephone," with one bishop whispering teachings in the ear of the next. Rather, through Apostolic Succession the bishops have been entrusted with the authority to interpret the content of Divine Revelation—both Scripture and Tradition. The teaching authority of the bishops is called the magisterium. Guided by the Holy Spirit, the bishops are able to constantly communicate the truth of revelation in a way that makes sense to people in every age. This means that the Gospel is never something old, obsolete, or irrelevant. Rather, the Word of God is alive.

> For the word of God is living and active, sharper than any two-edged sword, piercing to the division of soul and spirit, of joints and marrow, and discerning the thoughts and intentions of the heart. (Heb 4:12)

This understanding of Scripture is important, because it helps us see that the Word of God continues to speak to us today. It also reminds us that the way we talk about Scripture will change as the world changes. After all, the world is different today than it was in the year 1000, so the ways we talk about revelation need to change too. This is to say, if we're going to help people understand the truth about God in every age, we have to communicate that truth in a way that's relevant to that particular age. Truth never changes, but how we communicate that truth—the language and metaphors we use, or the points we emphasize—can . . . and often should.

History is about change: language, culture, economics, and politics all change through time. This means that while the truths of Revelation remain the same, the best way to communicate these truths changes through time. The history of the way that the bishops have talked about Divine Revelation is also part of Tradition. The Church goes through this process of constantly reflecting on who Jesus is and trying to understand more about him so that she can better communicate the truth to the people of each particular age. In doing so, the Church continues to learn more about Jesus. Guided by the Holy Spirit, the Church's understanding of its own teachings deepens. This is sometimes called the "Development of Doctrine," and it, too, is part of the Tradition. In short, Tradition is the Church's living transmission of the message of the Gospel. It is a dynamic, living thing that defies simple definitions.

Scripture and Tradition always go together, and together their content is called the Deposit of Faith. When the bishops exercise their teaching authority, they always draw from the Deposit of Faith. The Church doesn't make up new things. Rather, she constantly reaches back into the Deposit of Faith, pulls forward the truths of Divine Revelation, and presents them to the world in fresh ways. The Deposit of Faith, interpreted by the magisterium, makes God's Divine Revelation constantly available to us.

God's plan for our salvation includes both his telling us about who he is through Revelation and his giving us grace, especially through the sacraments. In the Eucharist, Jesus himself comes to us and unites us to himself. This combination of words and deeds is God's invitation to heaven. The Church calls this the Economy of Salvation. Both God's revelation and his grace come to us through the Church: The Church tells us what God has said and done, and it brings us the sacraments. The Church, therefore, continues to present to us God's invitation to heaven. We accept this invitation through faith. Faith is our response to God's offering of himself. It is our acceptance of a relationship with God.

SELECTED READING:
Second Vatican Council, Dogmatic Constitution on Divine
Revelation *Dei Verbum* (November 18, 1965), nos. 2–10

In His goodness and wisdom God chose to reveal Himself and to make known to us the hidden purpose of His will (see Eph. 1:9) by which through Christ, the Word made flesh, man might in the Holy Spirit have access to the Father and come to share in the divine nature (see Eph. 2:18; 2 Peter 1:4). Through this revelation, therefore, the invisible God (see Col. 1:15, 1 Tim. 1:17) out of the abundance of His love speaks to men as friends (see Ex. 33:11; John 15:14–15) and lives among them (see Bar. 3:38), so that He may invite and take them into fellowship with Himself. This plan of revelation is realized by deeds and words having an inner unity: the deeds wrought by God in the history of salvation manifest and confirm the teaching and realities signified by the words, while the words proclaim the deeds and clarify the mystery contained in them. By this revelation then, the deepest truth about God and the salvation of man shines out for our sake in Christ, who is both the mediator and the fullness of all revelation.

God, who through the Word creates all things (see John 1:3) and keeps them in existence, gives men an enduring witness to Himself in created realities (see Rom. 1:19–20). Planning to make known the

way of heavenly salvation, He went further and from the start manifested Himself to our first parents. Then after their fall His promise of
redemption aroused in them the hope of being saved (see Gen. 3:15)
and from that time on He ceaselessly kept the human race in His
care, to give eternal life to those who perseveringly do good in search
of salvation (see Rom. 2:6–7). Then, at the time He had appointed
He called Abraham in order to make of him a great nation (see Gen.
12:2). Through the patriarchs, and after them through Moses and
the prophets, He taught this people to acknowledge Himself the one
living and true God, provident father and just judge, and to wait for
the Savior promised by Him, and in this manner prepared the way
for the Gospel down through the centuries.

Then, after speaking in many and varied ways through the
prophets, "now at last in these days God has spoken to us in His Son"
(Heb. 1:1–2). For He sent His Son, the eternal Word, who enlight-
ens all men, so that He might dwell among men and tell them of the
innermost being of God (see John 1:1–18). Jesus Christ, therefore,
the Word made flesh, was sent as "a man to men." He "speaks the
words of God" (John 3:34), and completes the work of salvation
which His Father gave Him to do (see John 5:36; John 17:4). To see
Jesus is to see His Father (John 14:9). For this reason Jesus perfected
revelation by fulfilling it through his whole work of making Himself
present and manifesting Himself: through His words and deeds, His
signs and wonders, but especially through His death and glorious
resurrection from the dead and final sending of the Spirit of truth.
Moreover He confirmed with divine testimony what revelation proclaimed, that God is with us to free us from the darkness of sin and
death, and to raise us up to life eternal.

The Christian dispensation, therefore, as the new and definitive
covenant, will never pass away and we now await no further new
public revelation before the glorious manifestation of our Lord Jesus
Christ (see 1 Tim. 6:14 and Tit. 2:13).

"The obedience of faith" (Rom. 16:26; see 1:5; 2 Cor 10:5–6) "is
to be given to God who reveals, an obedience by which man commits
his whole self freely to God, offering the full submission of intel-

lect and will to God who reveals," and freely assenting to the truth revealed by Him. To make this act of faith, the grace of God and the interior help of the Holy Spirit must precede and assist, moving the heart and turning it to God, opening the eyes of the mind and giving "joy and ease to everyone in assenting to the truth and believing it." To bring about an ever deeper understanding of revelation the same Holy Spirit constantly brings faith to completion by His gifts.

Through divine revelation, God chose to show forth and communicate Himself and the eternal decisions of His will regarding the salvation of men. That is to say, He chose to share with them those divine treasures which totally transcend the understanding of the human mind.

As a sacred synod has affirmed, God, the beginning and end of all things, can be known with certainty from created reality by the light of human reason (see Rom. 1:20); but teaches that it is through His revelation that those religious truths which are by their nature accessible to human reason can be known by all men with ease, with solid certitude and with no trace of error, even in this present state of the human race.

In His gracious goodness, God has seen to it that what He had revealed for the salvation of all nations would abide perpetually in its full integrity and be handed on to all generations. Therefore Christ the Lord in whom the full revelation of the supreme God is brought to completion (see 2 Cor. 1:20; 3:13; 4:6), commissioned the Apostles to preach to all men that Gospel which is the source of all saving truth and moral teaching, and to impart to them heavenly gifts. This Gospel had been promised in former times through the prophets, and Christ Himself had fulfilled it and promulgated it with His lips. This commission was faithfully fulfilled by the Apostles who, by their oral preaching, by example, and by observances handed on what they had received from the lips of Christ, from living with Him, and from what He did, or what they had learned through the prompting of the Holy Spirit. The commission was fulfilled, too, by those Apostles and apostolic men who under the inspiration of the same Holy Spirit committed the message of salvation to writing.

But in order to keep the Gospel forever whole and alive within the Church, the Apostles left bishops as their successors, "handing over" to them "the authority to teach in their own place." This sacred tradition, therefore, and Sacred Scripture of both the Old and New Testaments are like a mirror in which the pilgrim Church on earth looks at God, from whom she has received everything, until she is brought finally to see Him as He is, face to face (see 1 John 3:2).

And so the apostolic preaching, which is expressed in a special way in the inspired books, was to be preserved by an unending succession of preachers until the end of time. Therefore the Apostles, handing on what they themselves had received, warn the faithful to hold fast to the traditions which they have learned either by word of mouth or by letter (see 2 Thess. 2:15), and to fight in defense of the faith handed on once and for all (see Jude 1:3). Now what was handed on by the Apostles includes everything which contributes toward the holiness of life and increase in faith of the peoples of God; and so the Church, in her teaching, life and worship, perpetuates and hands on to all generations all that she herself is, all that she believes.

This tradition which comes from the Apostles develops in the Church with the help of the Holy Spirit. For there is a growth in the understanding of the realities and the words which have been handed down. This happens through the contemplation and study made by believers, who treasure these things in their hearts (see Luke, 2:19, 51) through a penetrating understanding of the spiritual realities which they experience, and through the preaching of those who have received through Episcopal succession the sure gift of truth. For as the centuries succeed one another, the Church constantly moves forward toward the fullness of divine truth until the words of God reach their complete fulfillment in her.

The words of the holy fathers witness to the presence of this living tradition, whose wealth is poured into the practice and life of the believing and praying Church. Through the same tradition the Church's full canon of the sacred books is known, and the sacred writings themselves are more profoundly understood and unceasingly made active in her; and thus God, who spoke of old, uninterruptedly converses with the bride of His beloved Son; and the Holy Spirit, through whom the living voice of the Gospel resounds in the Church, and through her, in the world, leads unto all truth those who believe and makes the word of Christ dwell abundantly in them (see Col. 3:16).

Hence there exists a close connection and communication between sacred tradition and Sacred Scripture. For both of them, flowing from the same divine wellspring, in a certain way merge into a unity and tend toward the same end. For Sacred Scripture is the word of God inasmuch as it is consigned to writing under the inspiration of the divine Spirit, while sacred tradition takes the word of God entrusted by Christ the Lord and the Holy Spirit to the Apostles, and hands it on to their successors in its full purity, so that led by the light of the Spirit of truth, they may in proclaiming it preserve this word of God faithfully, explain it, and make it more widely known. Consequently it is not from Sacred Scripture alone that the Church draws her certainty about everything which has been revealed. Therefore both sacred tradition and Sacred Scripture are to be accepted and venerated with the same sense of loyalty and reverence.

Sacred tradition and Sacred Scripture form one sacred deposit of the word of God, committed to the Church. Holding fast to this deposit the entire holy people united with their shepherds remain always steadfast in the teaching of the Apostles, in the common life, in the breaking of the bread and in prayers (see Acts 2:42, Greek text), so that holding to, practicing and professing the heritage of the faith, it becomes on the part of the bishops and faithful a single common effort.

But the task of authentically interpreting the word of God, whether written or handed on, has been entrusted exclusively to the living teaching office of the Church, whose authority is exercised in the name of Jesus Christ. This teaching office is not above the word of God, but serves it, teaching only what has been handed on, listening to it devoutly, guarding it scrupulously and explaining it faithfully in accord with a divine commission and with the help of the

Holy Spirit, it draws from this one deposit of faith everything which it presents for belief as divinely revealed.

It is clear, therefore, that sacred tradition, Sacred Scripture and the teaching authority of the Church, in accord with God's most wise design, are so linked and joined together that one cannot stand without the others, and that all together and each in its own way under the action of the one Holy Spirit contribute effectively to the salvation of souls.

QUESTIONS FOR REVIEW

1. Where do we encounter natural revelation?
2. Where do we encounter Divine Revelation?
3. What is the magisterium?
4. What is the Deposit of Faith?
5. What is meant by the phrase, "Development of Doctrine"?

QUESTIONS FOR DISCUSSION

1. When you look at the world around you—the stars, the countryside, forests, and oceans—what does it reveal to you about God? Do you see signs of him in his creation?
2. God has revealed himself to us. How do you reveal yourself to others? Why do you want others to know you?
3. Why do you think God has revealed himself to us? What does this tell you about God?

Chapter 2

Faith: The Response to God's Self-Revelation

ASSIGNED READING
Hebrews 11
John 11:17–27
Matthew 16:13–20
1 Peter 1:3–12
CCC 144–159

What Is Faith?

We encounter God's Word in Scripture, in Tradition, and most perfectly in the Eucharist. All these are encounters with God's generous self-giving. The human response to God's generosity is Faith.

The First Vatican Council (1870) defined faith as:

> a supernatural virtue by which we, with the aid and inspiration of the grace of God, believe that the things revealed by Him are true, not because the intrinsic truth of the revealed things has been perceived by the natural light of reason, but because of the

authority of God himself who reveals them, who can neither deceive nor be deceived.[1]

This is a pretty thick definition. We can boil it down to this: Faith is a gift from God that allows us to know God and conform our minds, hearts, and wills to him. Faith might seem like a difficult thing; conforming ourselves to God sounds very hard. But, a key part of the definition of faith, a part that is often overlooked, is that faith is a gift from God; it is a grace. All we have to do is accept the gift. We don't do it ourselves. In his encyclical *Lumen Fidei*, Pope Francis describes faith this way:

> The light of faith is unique, since it is capable of illuminating *every aspect* of human existence. A light this powerful cannot come from ourselves but from a more primordial source: in a word, it must come from God. Faith is born of an encounter with the living God who calls us and reveals his love, a love which precedes us and upon which we can lean for security and for building our lives. Transformed by this love, we gain fresh vision, new eyes to see; we realize that it contains a great promise of fulfillment, and that a vision of the future opens up before us.[2]

Faith is not a "blind leap." It is a transformative encounter with the living God. Like meeting a new friend, faith is meeting God, and the more our relationship with him grows, the more we are transformed.

Importantly, our faith is in God, who is a Trinity of Persons: Father, Son, and Holy Spirit. The Son is the Person of the Trinity we have seen. Two thousand years ago, in the land of Israel, the Son of God became a man. We call this the Incarnation, and it is the greatest possible gift. God doesn't ask us to believe in some impersonal force or some incomprehensible being living in a distant spiritual realm. Rather, we're asked to believe in a man who walked around and spoke to us, a man whom we know

---

[1] First Vatican Council, Dogmatic Constitution on the Catholic Faith *Dei Filius* (April 24, 1870), §3, in Vincent McNabb, ed., *The Decrees of the Vatican Council* (New York: Benziger Brothers, 1907).

[2] Pope Francis, Encyclical Letter on Faith *Lumen Fidei* (June 29, 2013), §4.

existed, and whose friends wrote down his words and actions, what he did and said. Our God took on our humanity. The Word of God became a man and told us about himself and about his Father. People touched him. They were his friends. And that's what he asks us to be as well. We are asked to accept the friendship of a man who is also God, to study his life and listen to his words, and to develop a personal relationship with him.

Through Jesus, we can also come to know the other Persons of the Trinity. Jesus himself told us that through him we can come to know God (Matt 11:27; Luke 10:22). Jesus tells us who God the Father is, and so Jesus is our path to him. Faith in Jesus is also sharing in his Spirit. It is through the action of the Holy Spirit, the Third Person of the Trinity, that we receive the gift of faith. The Holy Spirit constantly acts in our lives, helping us enter into a closer relationship with the Father and the Son. Faith in God, therefore, is always faith in the three Persons of the Trinity: the Father, the Son, and the Holy Spirit.

Faith and Reason

This faith of ours is never blind faith. It is always accompanied by reason. Reason is how we think about the things we know. Through the process of reasoning, we piece together different bits of information into a seamless whole and arrive at new knowledge. Here is a classic example of reasoning:

> I know that Socrates is a man;
> I know all men are mortal;
> Therefore, I know Socrates is mortal.

So, as that example helps us see, you may not have actually witnessed Socrates' death, but you can be sure of it nonetheless, through rational reflection on what you do know about Socrates and about men in general. That's what reason does for us. It takes the things we know, including our observations about the world around us, and shows us their connections and implications.

Despite what some people say, reason is perfectly compatible with the Christian faith. In fact, it's more than compatible; for a mature faith it's absolutely necessary. God reveals to us a great deal about himself, but we still have to think about and reflect upon that revelation in order to really know him. We have to take what God says about himself and what we know about the world and ourselves, and then we need to bring it all together. Reason makes it possible for us to do this. Because God made the physical world, including us, and because revelation is God telling us about himself, what we know through observation and reason can't be at odds with what we know through revelation—both reason and revelation are the work of the Creator of everything, God. How could they be in conflict? It's not rational.

The Church, therefore, has always taught that it would be a huge mistake to set aside one's reason and have "blind" faith in something that doesn't make sense. Instead, the Church invites us, as rational people, to meet and interact with a living God. Our faith is trust in God, a trust that we have because we learn to know him as a trustworthy person, which is a totally reasonable thing to do. Both faith and reason venture together on the path toward God.

Pope St. John Paul II expressed the harmony between faith and reason in his encyclical *Fides et Ratio*:

> Faith and reason are like two wings on which the human spirit rises to the contemplation of truth; and God has placed in the human heart a desire to know the truth—in a word, to know self—so that, by knowing and loving God, men and women may also come to the fullness of truth about themselves (cf. *Ex* 33:18; *Ps* 27:8–9; 63:2–3; *Jn* 14:8; *1 Jn* 3:2).[3]

Faith, therefore, is a certainty because it is an encounter, an experience of God. The Catechism puts it like this:

---

[3] John Paul II, Encyclical Letter on the Relationship Between Faith and Reason *Fides et Ratio* (September 14, 1998), introduction.

Faith is *certain*. It is more certain than all human knowledge because it is founded on the very word of God who cannot lie. To be sure, revealed truths can seem obscure to human reason and experience, but "the certainty that the divine light gives is greater than that which the light of natural reason gives" [St. Thomas Aquinas, *STh* II-II, 171, 5, obj.3]. "Ten thousand difficulties do not make one doubt" [John Henry Cardinal Newman, *Apologia pro vita sua* (London: Longman, 1878) 239]. (CCC 157)

Faith and Discipleship

What Does It Mean to Be a Disciple of Jesus?

Faith is not just something that happens in our minds. Our faith in Jesus Christ always leads to discipleship. But what does it mean to be a disciple?

A dictionary would tell you that a disciple is someone who accepts the doctrine of another and tries to help him spread that doctrine. Someone can be the disciple of a philosopher, for example, or of a political leader. Christian discipleship, however, goes beyond this definition. We *do* accept Christ's teaching, and we *do* try to help him spread it. However, as we have already seen, we don't "believe" in the teaching of Jesus like we might "believe" that a certain philosopher is right in his arguments. Rather, we have *faith* in Jesus, which we understand as a personal relationship with him as a Person. It's not just Jesus' teachings in which we "believe." We "believe" in *him*. We believe in everything he did and everything he is. We don't just respect him as a teacher; we love him as a person.

This leads to a discipleship that goes well beyond the dictionary's definition. Because we love Jesus, we want to be like him. Moreover, Jesus is the "perfect man" because he is the God who created man. He is a man who is the way all men are supposed to be. As we grow in our faith, as we learn more about him, and as we give more of ourselves to the relationship, holding back less and less for ourselves, we desire to become more like Jesus. Faith leads us to understand Jesus' perfection, not just in what he said, but in what he did.

Part of coming to understand this perfection is the desire to have it for ourselves; it's wanting to become perfect as Jesus is perfect, to become the way God made us to be. This is discipleship, and faith doesn't exist without it. Jesus is the model in all that he taught and all that he did. He humbled himself, he prayed, he taught, he suffered for the truth. Disciples are called to do all these things. When we do these things we become more like Jesus. We get closer to his perfection, and our relationship with him grows, so our faith is strengthened. Faith and discipleship are two sides of the same coin.

The Church's discipleship is one of the ways that the mission of Jesus continues in the world. Jesus lives on in the lives of the faithful. The Church teaches what Jesus taught and the Church does what Jesus did. In fact, through faith, which always includes discipleship, we become the adopted brothers and sisters of Jesus and a part of the life of the Trinity. This is really what the Church understands as our salvation. We are saved when the division that opened up between God and human beings after the sin of Adam and Eve is bridged.

Jesus is that bridge, and by becoming his disciples in faith, by conforming ourselves to him, can we gain "a real share in the life of the only Son" (CCC 654), a life in the unity of the Trinity. Conforming ourselves to him is not just believing a list of doctrines are true or even believing that a certain way of life is good. Such faith without works is dead (Jas 2:26). Rather, conforming ourselves to him, which is called discipleship and which results from true faith, always involves doing things in the world. Jesus, after all, did a great many things. In the Christian tradition, these actions are called works.

Discipleship Is Rooted in Love

What do these works or actions to which we are called look like? Answering that question starts with love. The central rule of discipleship is love, and so all works are rooted in love. Jesus loved his disciples to the end, even dying for them, which he said was proof of perfect love (John 15:13). He also passes on to us the love he receives from the Father. Love has no limit. There could never be "too many" people bound together in love—there is always room for one more! So, Jesus, who is eternally loved by the Father, extends that love to his disciples. This bond of love is the very bond that unites the three Persons of the Trinity, and so, by loving us, Jesus invites us into the life of the Trinity. We accept this invitation by returning Jesus' love and by loving one another. The Catechism puts it this way:

> By loving one another, the disciples imitate the love of Jesus, which they themselves receive. Whence Jesus says: "As the Father has loved me, so have I loved you; abide in my love." And again: "This is my commandment, that you love one another as I have loved you [Jn 15:9, 12]." (CCC 1823)

Jesus tells us in the Bible that all the commandments of the law—for example, the Ten Commandments—can be summed up in the commandments to love God and to love our neighbor (Matt 22:37–40). The actions of discipleship in the world—our works—are simply the actions of someone who loves God and his fellow human beings.

But what is love? In our culture, love is normally presented as a mushy romantic thing—like roses and hearts and valentines. Love is also presented as a feeling or an emotion. You love someone, according to our culture, when you really like them a lot and when they make you happy or they bring you pleasure. All this is a part of real love, but it's not the whole. It's incomplete. Real love is not about the lover but about the beloved. When you really love someone, you want what is good for them, and you want that because it is good for them. When you really love someone, if there is something that you have that you could give up in order to make them happy, including your life, you give it up. You do this because the other person's happiness is the thing that you want more than anything else. Real love is sacrificial.

This was the love Jesus had for us. This is to say that the ultimate image of love is not a silly red heart with an arrow through it; the ultimate image of love is the Cross. Discipleship is the call to love God and our fellow human beings. This is not soft and mushy. This is heroic. A disciple must be willing to pick up his own cross and follow Jesus (Matt 10:38; Mark 8:34; Luke 9:23).

SELECTED READING:

First Vatican Council, Dogmatic Constitution on the
Catholic Faith *Dei Filius* (April 24, 1870), chaps. 3 and 4

Since man is wholly dependent on God as his Creator and Lord, and
since created reason is completely subject to uncreated truth, we are
bound by faith to give full obedience of intellect and will to God who
reveals (can. 1). But the Catholic Church professes that this faith,
which "is the beginning of human salvation" (cf. n. 801), is a supernatural virtue by which we, with the aid and inspiration of the grace
of God, believe that the things revealed by Him are true, not because
the intrinsic truth of the revealed things has been perceived by the
natural light of reason, but because of the authority of God Himself
who reveals them, who can neither deceive nor be deceived (can. 2).
For, "faith is," as the Apostle testifies, "the substance of things to be
hoped for, the evidence of things that appear not" (Heb. 11:1).

However, in order that the "obedience" of our faith should be
"consonant with reason" (cf. Rom. 12:1), God has willed that to
the internal aids of the Holy Spirit there should be joined external
proofs of His revelation, namely: divine facts, especially miracles and
prophecies which, because they clearly show forth the omnipotence
and infinite knowledge of God, are most certain signs of a divine
revelation, and are suited to the intelligence of all (can. 3 and 4).
Wherefore, not only Moses and the prophets, but especially Christ
the Lord Himself, produced many genuine miracles and prophecies;
and we read concerning the apostles: "But they going forth preached
everywhere: the Lord working withal and confirming the word with
signs that followed" (Mark 16:20). And again it is written: "And we
have the more firm prophetical word: whereunto you do well to
attend, as to a light that shineth in a dark place" (2 Pet. 1:19).

Moreover, although the assent of faith is by no means a blind
movement of the intellect, nevertheless, no one can "assent to the
preaching of the Gospel," as he must to attain salvation, "without
the illumination and inspiration of the Holy Spirit, who gives to
all a sweetness in consenting to and believing in truth" (Council of

Orange, see n. 178 ff.). Wherefore, "faith" itself in itself, even if it "worketh not by charity" (cf. Gal. 5:6), is a gift of God, and its act is a work pertaining to salvation, by which man offers a free obedience to God Himself by agreeing to, and cooperating with His grace, which he could resist (cf. n. 797 f: can. 5).

Further, by divine and Catholic faith, all those things must be believed which are contained in the written word of God and in tradition, and those which are proposed by the Church, either in a solemn pronouncement or in her ordinary and universal teaching power, to be believed as divinely revealed.

But, since "without faith it is impossible to please God" (Heb. 11:6) and to attain to the fellowship of His sons, hence, no one is justified without it; nor will anyone attain eternal life except "he shall persevere unto the end on it" (Matt. 10:22; 24:13). Moreover, in order that we may satisfactorily perform the duty of embracing the true faith and of continuously persevering in it, God, through His only-begotten Son, has instituted the Church, and provided it with clear signs of His institution, so that it can be recognized by all as the guardian and teacher of the revealed word.

For, to the Catholic Church alone belong all those many and marvelous things which have been divinely arranged for the evident credibility of the Christian faith. But, even the Church itself by itself, because of its marvelous propagation, its exceptional holiness, and inexhaustible fruitfulness in all good works; because of its catholic unity and invincible stability, is a very great and perpetual motive of credibility, and an incontestable witness of its own divine mission.

By this it happens that the Church as "a standard set up unto the nations" (Isa. 11:12), both invites to itself those who have not yet believed, and makes its sons more certain that the faith, which they profess, rests on a very firm foundation. Indeed, an efficacious aid to this testimony has come from supernatural virtue. For, the most benign God both excites the erring by His grace and aids them so that they can "come to a knowledge of the truth" (1 Tim. 2:4), and also confirms in His grace those whom "He has called out of darkness into his marvelous light" (1 Pet. 2:9), so that they may persevere in this same light, not deserting if He be not deserted. . . . Wherefore, not at all equal is the condition of those, who, through the heavenly gift of faith, have adhered to the Catholic truth, and of those, who, led by human opinions, follow a false religion; for, those who have accepted the faith under the teaching power of the Church can never have a just cause of changing or doubting that faith (can. 6). Since this is so, "giving thanks to God the Father, who hath made us worthy to be partakers of the lot of the saints in light" (Col. 1:12), let us not neglect such salvation, but "looking on Jesus, the author and finisher of faith" (Heb. 12:2), "let us hold fast the confession of our hope without wavering" (Heb. 10:23).

By enduring agreement the Catholic Church has held and holds that there is a twofold order of knowledge, distinct not only in principle but also in object: (1) in principle, indeed, because we know in one way by natural reason, in another by divine faith; (2) in object, however, because, in addition to things to which natural reason can attain, mysteries hidden in God are proposed to us for belief which, had they not been divinely revealed, could not become known (can. 1). Wherefore, the Apostle, who testifies that God was known to the Gentiles "by the things that are made" (Rom. 1:20), nevertheless, when discoursing about grace and truth which "was made through Jesus Christ" (ct. John 1:17) proclaims: "We speak the wisdom of God in a mystery, a wisdom which is hidden, which God ordained before the world, unto our glory, which none of the princes of this world know. . . . But to us God hath revealed them by His Spirit. For the Spirit searcheth all things, yea the deep things of God" (1 Cor. 2:7, 8, 10). And the Only-begotten Himself "confesses to the Father, because He hath hid these things from the wise and prudent, and hath revealed them to little ones" (cf. Matt. 11:25).

And, indeed, reason illustrated by faith, when it zealously, piously, and soberly seeks, attains with the help of God some understanding of the mysteries, and that a most profitable one, not only from the analogy of those things which it knows naturally, but also from the connection of the mysteries among themselves and with the last end of man; nevertheless, it is never capable of perceiving those mysteries in the way it does the truths which constitute its own proper object. For, divine mysteries by their nature exceed the created intellect so much that, even when handed down by revelation and accepted by faith, they nevertheless remain covered by the veil of faith itself, and wrapped in a certain mist, as it were, as long as in this mortal life, "we are absent from the Lord: for we walk by faith and not by sight" (2 Cor. 5:6 f.).

But, although faith is above reason, nevertheless, between faith and reason no true dissension can ever exist, since the same God, who reveals mysteries and infuses faith, has bestowed on the human soul the light of reason; moreover, God cannot deny Himself, nor ever contradict truth with truth. But, a vain appearance of such a contradiction arises chiefly from this, that either the dogmas of faith have not been understood and interpreted according to the mind of the Church, or deceitful opinions are considered as the determinations of reason. Therefore, "every assertion contrary to the truth illuminated by faith, we define to be altogether false" (Lateran Council V, see n. 738).

Further, the Church which, together with the apostolic duty of teaching, has received the command to guard the deposit of faith, has also, from divine Providence, the right and duty of proscribing "knowledge falsely so called" (1 Tim. 6:20), "lest anyone be cheated by philosophy and vain deceit" (cf. Col. 2:8; can. 2). Wherefore, all faithful Christians not only are forbidden to defend opinions of this sort, which are known to be contrary to the teaching of faith, especially if they have been condemned by the Church, as the legitimate conclusions of science, but they shall be altogether bound to hold them rather as errors, which present a false appearance of truth.

And, not only can faith and reason never be at variance with one another, but they also bring mutual help to each other, since right reasoning demonstrates the basis of faith and, illumined by its light, perfects the knowledge of divine things, while faith frees and protects reason from errors and provides it with manifold knowledge. Wherefore, the Church is so far from objecting to the culture of the human arts and sciences, that it aids and promotes this cultivation in many ways. For, it is not ignorant of, nor does it despise the advantages flowing therefrom into human life; nay, it confesses that, just as they have come forth from "God, the Lord of knowledge" (1 Kings 2:3), so, if rightly handled, they lead to God by the aid of His grace. And it (the Church) does not forbid disciplines of this kind, each in its own sphere, to use its own principles and its own method; but, although recognizing this freedom, it continually warns them not to fall into errors by opposition to divine doctrine, nor, having transgressed their own proper limits, to be busy with and to disturb those matters which belong to faith.

For, the doctrine of faith which God revealed has not been handed down as a philosophic invention to the human mind to be perfected, but has been entrusted as a divine deposit to the Spouse of Christ, to be faithfully guarded and infallibly interpreted. Hence, also, that understanding of its sacred dogmas must be perpetually retained, which Holy Mother Church has once declared; and there must never be recession from that meaning under the specious name of a deeper understanding (can. 3). "Therefore . . . let the understanding, the knowledge, and wisdom of individuals as of all, of one man as of the whole Church, grow and progress strongly with the passage of the ages and the centuries; but let it be solely in its own genus, namely in the same dogma, with the same sense and the same understanding."

QUESTIONS FOR REVIEW

1. Define "faith."
2. Is faith something we can earn? If not, how do we get it?
3. What is the relationship between faith and reason?
4. Define "disciple."
5. What is the difference between being a disciple of Jesus and being a disciple of anyone else?

QUESTIONS FOR DISCUSSION

1. Are you surprised to hear that the Church discourages blind faith? Why or why not?
2. How does the Church's understanding of love differ from the world's understanding of love? Which kind of love do you think is more difficult? Why?
3. Who is someone you know that truly lives as a disciple of Christ? What makes their witness powerful?

Chapter 3

Discipleship in the Church

ASSIGNED READING
1 Corinthians 12:12–31
CCC 84–90

Grace

Discipleship sounds like a terribly hard thing. Who but Jesus is strong enough to love his enemies to the point of dying for them on the Cross? The truth is, no one is strong enough on their own. Luckily, we are not on our own. We have a great deal of help.

Jesus' mission was to pour God's grace into the world. Grace is free help from God. Without it, true discipleship would be impossible. Fortunately for us, God gives each of us all the grace and all the help we need in order to fulfill the call to discipleship. The question is whether we respond to this grace and accept the help. Even here, though, when it comes to our response, we have help. We have the Church. Jesus founded the Church to help us respond properly to God's offer of grace.

The chief way in which grace is given to humanity is through the sacraments of the Church. The sacraments of Christian initiation are Baptism, Confirmation, and the Eucharist. These three sacraments are the means through which God gives us the grace necessary to fulfill our vocation as disciples. Baptism fills the void left in each of us by original sin and makes us members of the Church, the Body of Christ. Confirmation strengthens us as we reach maturity, giving us the grace necessary to become full disciples. The Eucharist is the actual Sacrament of Communion. It binds us together and it binds us with Jesus, making the Church his Body. The Eucharist is a constant source of grace that makes the Christian life in this world possible. The importance of the sacraments cannot be overestimated. Without them, we can't be true disciples.

Community

The Church dispenses God's grace through the sacraments, and the faithful are bound together through them. Through the grace of the sacraments, we receive the means to live as disciples, which means the Church is fundamentally a community of disciples. Christians are bound together through faith and through our love for each other. Importantly, when it comes to discipleship, this community isn't an extra or an add-on. It is essential. We need this community—we need the Church—in order to become disciples. After all, love is impossible unless there is more than one person. Love is something that people do together, as a community. Not only are other people necessary for love to have any meaning, but there is no greater help in learning how to love than to be loved by someone. Experiencing love and seeing people love each other is a part of learning how to be a disciple.

Most people first encounter love in their families. The love parents have for their child is similar to both the love that God has for each of us and the love that we are supposed to have for each other. Children learn from the love of their parents. In a similar way, the Church is like one large family. We are all the adopted sons and daughters of God, and as one big family we learn about how to love from each other. Living your life in a community of disciples helps you become a better disciple. This is especially true when you consider that the community of the faithful to which we belong has two thousand years' worth of experience in the pursuit of discipleship. The devotions and prayers of the Church, which have developed over the centuries, contain great wisdom, and these practices and prayers are made available to us, along with a community that knows how to use them, so that we can progress in the spiritual life.

In addition to the lives of the disciples around us, we also have the help of those nearly perfect disciples: the saints. We see in the saints that heroic love is possible. They model for us what discipleship looks like and give us confidence that we, too, can accomplish the task. If they could be saints, so can we! As Pope Benedict XVI has exhorted young people: "Dare to be glowing saints, in whose eyes and hearts the love of Christ beams and who thus bring light to the world."[1]

Conforming our lives to those of our fellow Christians can help us conform our lives to the life of Christ. This can sound strange to some of us, as we have been raised in a culture where conformity is often treated as a bad thing. Most of us like to think of ourselves as individuals, doing things our own way and living life by our own rules. We've been told that we're supposed to express our individuality by refusing to "conform" or refusing to play by anyone else's playbook. The problem with this is twofold.

First, we can't avoid conforming. Human beings are social by nature. We always live in community, and those communities always grow together: that is, the members of communities become more like each other. This is just obvious. Think about how, as you and your friends spend more time together, you start using the same figures of speech, even adopting the same mannerisms. Not conforming ourselves to others is not really an option for us. In fact, when we look around us, we see that "refusing to conform" really just entails conforming to a community of "non-conformists," who pretty much see the world in the same way, wear the same clothes, listen to the same music, and watch the same movies. The question is not whether or not to conform. The question is to what we will conform. Will we conform to a community based on love, or will we conform to a community based on envy, competition, and pride?

The second mistake made by those who are against the general idea

---

[1] Pope Benedict XVI, Address during the Vigil with Young People, (Freiburg im Breisgau, Germany, September 24, 2011), https://w2.vatican.va/content/benedict-xvi/en/speeches/2011/september/documents/hf_ben-xvi_spe_20110924_vigil-freiburg.html.

of conforming is the belief that you lose your individuality when you conform yourself to others. This isn't the case with Christianity. The Church is the Body of Christ, and it has many members; it is made up of many individuals, who are all loved by God for who we are. This is why discipleship can't lead us to become less of who we are. Far from it! For who we are is exactly who is loved by God! For this reason, conformity to the law of love in the Church allows us to become fully who we are. When we realize that God loves us for us, for who he made us to be, we can stop trying to be someone else. Likewise, when we realize that our fellow disciples love us the way God made us to be, we can stop trying to be the way the world tells us we should be. At the same time, when we love others, our personality is fully alive because we were made by God to love each other. Christian discipleship is not at odds with us as individual persons. In fact, conforming to the life of the faithful is an act of liberation.

Our fellow Christians, however, including the saints, are more than just good models for us to follow. They also pray for us to God. The prayers of the Church are especially listened to by God and should never be underestimated.

As we have seen, being a disciple means being a member of the Church, which is the Mystical Body of Christ. The Church gives us the sacraments, and it gives us a community of faith and love—both necessary helps in our own journey. The Church also communicates to us what God has told us about himself. Our faith in Jesus is rooted in a personal relationship with him, but the particular knowledge of what is true about him and about his teaching comes to us through the Church—which exists to continue Jesus' mission on Earth.

When we listen to the teachings of Jesus, it is his Church who is pronouncing them. Rather than just handing us a book and saying, "Good luck!" the Church teaches us about Jesus: about who he is and about how we ought to come to know him more completely. The Church gives us the definitive interpretation of both Scripture and Tradition. The doctrines of the Church are therefore a necessary part of our journey to faithful discipleship. Without them, we wouldn't know in whom we're supposed to believe—we wouldn't know who Jesus is, and we wouldn't know what he asks us to do. As we have already mentioned, this teaching function of the Church is guided by the Holy Spirit and is called the magisterium.

Guidance

The Church also helps us through its precepts—its rules and moral teachings concerning right and wrong. In the popular culture, the Church is often presented as authoritarian, and Christianity is often presented as just a big list of things you're not allowed to do. This is a total mischaracterization. The Church gives us rules for living a life of authentic discipleship. It does this because we're not yet perfect and need help. Our faith is not perfect, our knowledge of Jesus is not perfect, and we have not yet become the masters of ourselves. Accordingly, we don't yet do the right thing simply because it is the right thing. We need help!

Because Jesus loves us, because he wants us to progress in our faith and grow closer to him and to become more perfect disciples, he gave his Church the authority to make rules for us and guide us to live a moral life. These rules that the Church makes for the faithful are rooted in the law of love and are aimed at guiding us ever closer to Jesus. In essence, the Church takes the law of love and translates it into particular guidelines for particular situations in the world in which we live. This is a great gift from God, and when we follow the Church's teachings, we grow in faith and holiness. Then, as we grow, the teachings and the rules become easier to follow. This is because they are less and less at odds with who we are. Eventually, the rules became the same as what we already want to do and we stop thinking of them as rules at all.

Here is an example: The Church tells us that we have to go to Mass every Sunday. This is a rule. We might start out going to Mass every Sunday because of this rule. But what happens at Mass? We hear the Word of God proclaimed. We associate with our fellow Christians and grow in community. And we are united sacramentally with both them and with God in the Eucharist. All this helps us grow in discipleship. Eventually, we stop thinking about the Church's rule about going to Mass every Sunday because we wouldn't dream of missing Mass; in fact, we probably want to go more often, maybe even every day! The rules and moral teachings of the Church are all like this. The ones we find difficult are the most important ones because they point out the places where we need to grow the most.

Other aspects of discipleship are similar. For example, we are called to share our faith with the world. This is called evangelization. This is what Jesus did, and we need to be like Jesus. Evangelization, however, can be a very difficult thing to do. It can be hard to talk to people about Jesus because we don't know if we will be able to express the truth clearly, we don't know how they will respond, and we don't know whether they will stop liking us. But a remarkable thing happens as you progress in the life of discipleship: sharing the truth about Jesus becomes easier in several ways.

First, your life itself becomes a form of evangelization. The more like Jesus you become, the more your everyday life teaches the people around you about him. When they see you, they get the best lesson possible about who Jesus is. Second, as your trust in Jesus deepens, you will become more and more confident in speaking about him. Trust is the foundation of any good relationship, and trust leads to confidence. As St. Paul writes, "I can do all things in him who strengthens me" (Phil 4:13). Discipleship also leads us to worry less about what people might think. It helps us understand that we just need to share what we know and feel, talking about our friendship with Jesus, and trust him. Anyone can do this. Finally, part of the life of a disciple is the study of the faith. As you learn more about Christianity it will become easier to share. Ultimately, being a good evangelizer just grows naturally out of a life of faithful discipleship.

Faith and Religion

The Church, for its part, is necessary for a life of discipleship. What it gives us—the sacraments, community, doctrine, precepts and moral code—are all necessary parts of living a Christian life. They are the help God gives us to tackle the challenges of discipleship. The Church also shows us how to worship God. When we join our worship of God with that of the Church, especially in the Mass, we are uniting our voice of praise to the voices of all the billions of Christians who are alive or who have ever lived or whoever will live. Even more amazingly, Jesus told us that when two or three of us are gathered together, he will be there (Matt 18:20). In the Catholic Church, when we gather for Mass, Jesus is completely present, in his Body, Blood, Soul, and Divinity.

All of this together—sacraments, community, doctrine, precepts, and worship—make up the Catholic religion. Religion is different but very closely related to faith. Both faith and religion are gifts from God. Basically, faith compels us to be disciples, and religion shows us how.

Every Sunday at Mass, we gather together as a community made up of people who share the gift of faith. We are all in the process of living lives of committed discipleship—this is where faith and religion intersect. In our day, some people claim that it is better to be "spiritual" without being "religious." Some have gone so far as to claim that Jesus taught against religion. But, as Father Robert Barron explains:

> The same Jesus who railed against the hypocritical legalism of the Pharisees also said, "I have come not to abolish the law but to fulfill it." And the same Jesus who threatened to tear down the Temple in Jerusalem also promised "in three days to rebuild it." The point is this: Jesus certainly criticized—even bitterly so— the corruptions in the institutional religion of his time, but he by no means called for its wholesale dismantling. He was, in point of fact, a loyal, observant, law-abiding Jew. What he affected was a transfiguration of the best of that classical Israelite religion—Temple, law, priesthood, sacrifice, covenant, etc.—into the institutions, sacraments, practices and structures of his Mystical Body, the Church.[2]

---

[2] Bishop Robert Baron, "Why Jesus and Religion Are Like Two Peas in a Pod," *Word on Fire*, January 18, 2012, https://www.wordonfire.org/resources/article/why-jesus-and-religion-are-like-two-peas-in-a-pod/432/.

Faith and religion are distinct, but they are essentially connected because of Jesus' universal mission: "And I, when I am lifted up from the earth, will draw all men to myself" (John 12:32).

The Fullness of Revelation in the Catholic Church

Each of us are called to communion with God and with each other. Communities are not optional; they are a part of being human. Look at Jesus. He was the perfect human, and he was a member of the Jewish people. He had a family, and he brought together and lived with a community of disciples. God does not want us to be less than human; he wants us to be *perfectly* human, like Jesus, and humans live not as individuals but in communities. The Church is his community. It is a divine communion of living people, with rules, rituals, customs, and everything else that characterizes any group of people gathered together with a common goal. As such, it reinforces the social side of humanity. This is why the central act of the Catholic faith is Holy Communion—that is, holy "common-union," expressed intimately with God and the community.

This communion, in turn, gives us the spiritual strength to make a difference in our lives and in our community. It's no coincidence that the Catholic Church is the largest charitable institution in the world. Our sacramental life empowers us to live our daily lives in such a way that we are constantly seeking to better the lives of those around us. We all are called to be living witnesses to the Gospel and, as St. Paul says, to "walk in a manner worthy of the calling to which you have been called, with all lowliness and meekness, with patience, forbearing one another in love, eager to maintain the unity of the Spirit in the bond of peace" (Eph 4:1–3).

But what makes our "common-union" different from non-Catholic churches? What is the communion that Jesus lays out in the Gospels? Which church does Jesus found? Of course we believe it is the Catholic Church, but more than this, it is only in the Catholic Church that we can find all the helps for discipleship named above in their fullness. It is only in the Catholic Church that we can find all the gifts that God wishes to give to the Church.

Christ has given everything to the Catholic Church because he is our founder and he has gathered us all into one community—the Body of Christ.

It is the unity of faith and our common baptism which marks the unity of the Church, "There is one body and one Spirit, just as you were called to the one hope that belongs to your call, one Lord, one faith, one baptism, one God and Father of us all, who is above all and through all and in all" (Eph 4:4–6). This unity is protected and handed on by the ministry of the pope and the other bishops, who shepherd the community of the faithful. Our common faith, our communion in and through the sacraments, and that communion expressed in union with the pope, make the Catholic Church stand out as the true Church of Christ.

The Catholic Church is Jesus' gift to the world to communicate himself. The Catholic Church is the continuation of his mission to the world, and that mission, in a word, is discipleship. Discipleship is not an optional way of life or one that only applies to priests and nuns. Jesus calls us to "Go therefore and make disciples of all nations . . ." (Matt 28:19). St. Paul summarized the goal of this mission of discipleship when he wrote: "that at the name of Jesus every knee should bow, in heaven and on earth and under the earth, and every tongue confess that Jesus Christ is Lord, to the glory of God the Father" (Phil 2:10–11).

In Part II, we will take a look at the Gospels and how Jesus' ministry fulfills the Scriptures and founds the Church for the building up of God's kingdom.

SELECTED READING:
Second Vatican Council, Dogmatic Constitution on the Church *Lumen Gentium* (November 21, 1964), nos. 39–42

The Church, whose mystery is being set forth by this Sacred Synod, is believed to be indefectibly holy. Indeed Christ, the Son of God, who with the Father and the Spirit is praised as "uniquely holy," loved the

Church as His bride, delivering Himself up for her. He did this that He might sanctify her. He united her to Himself as His own body and brought it to perfection by the gift of the Holy Spirit for God's glory. Therefore in the Church, everyone whether belonging to the hierarchy, or being cared for by it, is called to holiness, according to the saying of the Apostle: "For this is the will of God, your sanctification." However, this holiness of the Church is unceasingly manifested, and must be manifested, in the fruits of grace which the Spirit produces in the faithful; it is expressed in many ways in individuals, who in their walk of life, tend toward the perfection of charity, thus causing the edification of others; in a very special way this (holiness) appears in the practice of the counsels, customarily called "evangelical." This practice of the counsels, under the impulsion of the Holy Spirit, undertaken by many Christians, either privately or in a Church-approved condition or state of life, gives and must give in the world an outstanding witness and example of this same holiness.

The Lord Jesus, the divine Teacher and Model of all perfection, preached holiness of life to each and every one of His disciples of every condition. He Himself stands as the author and consummator of this holiness of life: "Be you therefore perfect, even as your heavenly Father is perfect." Indeed He sent the Holy Spirit upon all men that He might move them inwardly to love God with their whole heart and their whole soul, with all their mind and all their strength and that they might love each other as Christ loves them. The followers of Christ are called by God, not because of their works, but according to His own purpose and grace. They are justified in the Lord Jesus, because in the baptism of faith they truly become sons of God and sharers in the divine nature. In this way they are really made holy. Then too, by God's gift, they must hold on to and complete in their lives this holiness they have received. They are warned by the Apostle to live "as becomes saints," and to put on "as God's chosen ones, holy and beloved a heart of mercy, kindness, humility, meekness, patience," and to possess the fruit of the Spirit in holiness. Since truly we all offend in many things we all need God's mercies continually and we all must daily pray: "Forgive us our debts."

Thus it is evident to everyone, that all the faithful of Christ of whatever rank or status, are called to the fullness of the Christian life and to the perfection of charity; by this holiness as such a more human manner of living is promoted in this earthly society. In order that the faithful may reach this perfection, they must use their strength accordingly as they have received it, as a gift from Christ. They must follow in His footsteps and conform themselves to His image seeking the will of the Father in all things. They must devote themselves with all their being to the glory of God and the service of their neighbor. In this way, the holiness of the People of God will grow into an abundant harvest of good, as is admirably shown by the life of so many saints in Church history.

The classes and duties of life are many, but holiness is one—that sanctity which is cultivated by all who are moved by the Spirit of God, and who obey the voice of the Father and worship God the Father in spirit and in truth. These people follow the poor Christ, the humble and cross-bearing Christ in order to be worthy of being sharers in His glory. Every person must walk unhesitatingly according to his own personal gifts and duties in the path of living faith, which arouses hope and works through charity.

In the first place, the shepherds of Christ's flock must holily and eagerly, humbly and courageously carry out their ministry, in imitation of the eternal high Priest, the Shepherd and Guardian of our souls. They ought to fulfill this duty in such a way that it will be the principal means also of their own sanctification. Those chosen for the fullness of the priesthood are granted the ability of exercising the perfect duty of pastoral charity by the grace of the sacrament of Orders. This perfect duty of pastoral charity is exercised in every form of episcopal care and service, prayer, sacrifice and preaching. By this same sacramental grace, they are given the courage necessary to lay down their lives for their sheep, and the ability of promoting greater holiness in the Church by their daily example, having become a pattern for their flock.

Priests, who resemble bishops to a certain degree in their participation of the sacrament of Orders, form the spiritual crown of the bishops. They participate in the grace of their office and they should grow daily in their love of God and their neighbor by the exercise of their office through Christ, the eternal and unique Mediator. They should preserve the bond of priestly communion, and they should abound in every spiritual good and thus present to all men a living witness to God. All this they should do in emulation of those priests who often, down through the course of the centuries, left an outstanding example of the holiness of humble and hidden service. Their praise lives on in the Church of God. By their very office of praying and offering sacrifice for their own people and the entire people of God, they should rise to greater holiness. Keeping in mind what they are doing and imitating what they are handling, these priests, in their apostolic labors, rather than being ensnared by perils and hardships, should rather rise to greater holiness through these perils and hardships. They should ever nourish and strengthen their action from an abundance of contemplation, doing all this for the comfort of the entire Church of God. All priests, and especially those who are called "diocesan priests," due to the special title of their ordination, should keep continually before their minds the fact that their faithful loyalty toward and their generous cooperation with their bishop is of the greatest value in their growth in holiness.

Ministers of lesser rank are also sharers in the mission and grace of the Supreme Priest. In the first place among these ministers are deacons, who, in as much as they are dispensers of Christ's mysteries and servants of the Church, should keep themselves free from every vice and stand before men as personifications of goodness and friends of God. Clerics, who are called by the Lord and are set aside as His portion in order to prepare themselves for the various ministerial offices under the watchful eye of spiritual shepherds, are bound to bring their hearts and minds into accord with this special election (which is theirs). They will accomplish this by their constancy in prayer, by their burning love, and by their unremitting recollection of whatever is true, just and of good repute. They will accomplish all this for the glory and honor of God. Besides these already named, there are also laymen, chosen of God and called by the bishop. These laymen spend themselves completely in apostolic labors, working the Lord's field with much success.

Furthermore, married couples and Christian parents should follow their own proper path (to holiness) by faithful love. They should sustain one another in grace throughout the entire length of their lives. They should embue their offspring, lovingly welcomed as God's gift, with Christian doctrine and the evangelical virtues. In this manner, they offer all men the example of unwearying and generous love; in this way they build up the brotherhood of charity; in so doing, they stand as the witnesses and cooperators in the fruitfulness of Holy Mother Church; by such lives, they are a sign and a participation in that very love, with which Christ loved His Bride and for which He delivered Himself up for her. A like example, but one given in a different way, is that offered by widows and single people, who are able to make great contributions toward holiness and apostolic endeavor in the Church. Finally, those who engage in labor—and frequently it is of a heavy nature—should better themselves by their human labors. They should be of aid to their fellow citizens. They should raise all of society, and even creation itself, to a better mode of existence. Indeed, they should imitate by their lively charity, in their joyous hope and by their voluntary sharing of each others' burdens, the very Christ who plied His hands with carpenter's tools and Who in union with His Father, is continually working for the salvation of all men. In this, then, their daily work they should climb to the heights of holiness and apostolic activity.

May all those who are weighed down with poverty, infirmity and sickness, as well as those who must bear various hardships or who suffer persecution for justice sake—may they all know they are united with the suffering Christ in a special way for the salvation of the world. The Lord called them blessed in His Gospel and they are those whom "the God of all graces, who has called us unto His eternal glory in Christ Jesus, will Himself, after we have suffered a little while, perfect, strengthen and establish."

Finally all Christ's faithful, whatever be the conditions, duties and circumstances of their lives—and indeed through all these, will daily increase in holiness, if they receive all things with faith from the hand of their heavenly Father and if they cooperate with the divine will. In this temporal service, they will manifest to all men the love with which God loved the world.

"God is love, and he who abides in love, abides in God and God in Him." But, God pours out his love into our hearts through the Holy Spirit, Who has been given to us; thus the first and most necessary gift is love, by which we love God above all things and our neighbor because of God. Indeed, in order that love, as good seed may grow and bring forth fruit in the soul, each one of the faithful must willingly hear the Word of God and accept His Will, and must complete what God has begun by their own actions with the help of God's grace. These actions consist in the use of the sacraments and in a special way the Eucharist, frequent participation in the sacred action of the Liturgy, application of oneself to prayer, self-abnegation, lively fraternal service and the constant exercise of all the virtues. For charity, as the bond of perfection and the fullness of the law, rules over all the means of attaining holiness and gives life to these same means. It is charity which guides us to our final end. It is the love of God and the love of one's neighbor which points out the true disciple of Christ.

Since Jesus, the Son of God, manifested His charity by laying down His life for us, so too no one has greater love than he who lays down his life for Christ and His brothers. From the earliest times, then, some Christians have been called upon—and some will always be called upon—to give the supreme testimony of this love to all men, but especially to persecutors. The Church, then, considers martyrdom as an exceptional gift and as the fullest proof of love. By martyrdom a disciple is transformed into an image of his Master by freely accepting death for the salvation of the world—as well as his conformity to Christ in the shedding of his blood. Though few are presented such an opportunity, nevertheless all must be prepared to confess Christ before men. They must be prepared to make this profession of faith even in the midst of persecutions, which will never be lacking to the Church, in following the way of the cross.

Likewise, the holiness of the Church is fostered in a special way by the observance of the counsels proposed in the Gospel by Our Lord to His disciples. An eminent position among these is held by virginity or the celibate state. This is a precious gift of divine grace given by the Father to certain souls, whereby they may devote themselves to God alone the more easily, due to an undivided heart. This perfect continency, out of desire for the kingdom of heaven, has always been held in particular honor in the Church. The reason for this was and is that perfect continency for the love of God is an incentive to charity, and is certainly a particular source of spiritual fecundity in the world.

The Church continually keeps before it the warning of the Apostle which moved the faithful to charity, exhorting them to experience personally what Christ Jesus had known within Himself. This was the same Christ Jesus, who "emptied Himself, taking the nature of a slave . . . becoming obedient to death," and because of us "being rich, he became poor." Because the disciples must always offer an imitation of and a testimony to the charity and humility of Christ, Mother Church rejoices at finding within her bosom men and women who very closely follow their Saviour who debased Himself to our comprehension. There are some who, in their freedom as sons of God, renounce their own wills and take upon themselves the state of poverty. Still further, some become subject of their own accord to another man, in the matter of perfection for love of God. This is beyond the measure of the commandments, but is done in order to become more fully like the obedient Christ.

Therefore, all the faithful of Christ are invited to strive for the holiness and perfection of their own proper state. Indeed they have an obligation to so strive. Let all then have care that they guide aright their own deepest sentiments of soul. Let neither the use of the things of this world nor attachment to riches, which is against the spirit of evangelical poverty, hinder them in their quest for perfect love. Let them heed the admonition of the Apostle to those who use this world; let them not come to terms with this world; for this world, as we see it, is passing away.

QUESTIONS FOR REVIEW

1. What is grace?
2. What is the primary way grace comes to us?
3. How do the saints help us in the journey of discipleship?
4. What are the precepts of the Church?
5. How does the Church help us grow closer to Jesus?

QUESTIONS FOR DISCUSSION

1. Is there a saint whose life you find particularly inspiring? If so, who and why? Have you ever asked this saint for help?
2. Do you ever worry that having a relationship with Jesus will make you "less you"? Why or why not?
3. How, in the past, has your community of friends helped you to be a better person? Has your community of friends ever caused you to something that didn't reflect who God made you to be? What does this tell you about the importance of community?

Part II

Jesus Christ's Revelation about God

Faith, as we have seen, is our response to God's invitation to enter into a relationship with him and become his disciple. Ultimately, it is an encounter with the person of Jesus Christ. In Part II, we will discuss what Jesus Christ reveals to us about God. Through him we come to know the Father and the Holy Spirit, and through our faith in him we are formed as disciples and enter into loving relationship with each other. Jesus is at the very center of our relationship with God.

When the Son became a man through the Incarnation, God made his invitation to faith clear: "The time is fulfilled, and the kingdom of God is at hand; repent, and believe in the gospel" (Mark 1:15). The Incarnation completes the message that God had been communicating throughout salvation history. Christ is the fullness of divine Revelation. There is nothing to add because Jesus is "God with us" (Matt 1:23). St. Paul writes:

> But when the time had fully come, God sent forth his Son, born of woman, born under the law, to redeem those who were under the law, so that we might receive adoption as sons. And because you are sons, God has sent the Spirit of his Son into our hearts, crying, "Abba! Father!" So through God you are no longer a slave but a son, and if a son then an heir. (Gal 4:4–7)

Chapter 1

Son of God, Son of Mary

ASSIGNED READING
Luke 1:26–56
Luke 2:1–21
CCC 721–724

The question guiding this course on Christology is: "Who is Jesus Christ?" The answer to this question is the heart of all Christian doctrine. In a very real way, all of Christian theology is an attempt to answer this question, and it's not a simple question to answer, for Jesus Christ is the very center of history and the very center of all creation; he is the one through whom everything was made and to whom everything points. Jesus is God, the I AM, the Alpha and the Omega, the one who is and who was and who is to come (Rev 1:8). He also was born of a woman, talked to us, and died on a cross. He is, the Bible tells us, Emmanuel, which means "God-with-us."

This is the greatest of mysteries. Two thousand years after the Incarnation happened, we often take it for granted, but it would be impossible to exaggerate the significance of God himself becoming a human being. Jesus Christ had God as his Father and a human being, Mary, as his mother. Jesus can truly be called the Son of God, for he came from God, and he can truly be called the Son of Mary, for he took his humanity from her. So, Jesus is really a man and really God. He has a human nature and a divine nature, and yet he is one person: one divine person.

Mary, then, we can say, is literally the Mother of God. For this reason, the Blessed Mother has always held a special place in the heart of Christians. Her faithful response to God's invitation was crucial in the economy of salvation. Moreover, as Mary's Son, Jesus fulfills the *Protoevangelium* by which God announced to Adam and Eve that he would bring about redemption through another man and woman. This is why the Fathers of the Church call Jesus the "New Adam" and Mary the "New Eve."

At the same time, as the Son of God, Jesus is the second Person of the Trinity. In fact, he is the divine *Logos* or Word. He reveals all there is to reveal about God not only through his speech but also through his deeds, the things he did. Christ's communication of who God is and what he wants from us is not just found in his powerful sermons and parables, it is also in the things he did. It is in the path of his life, from a baby in a stable, to the quiet life as a carpenter, to his ministry, betrayal, and death.

Through all this—through his Incarnation, life, death, and Resurrection—Jesus Christ changed human history forever. Everything that happened before the Incarnation was preparation for it, and everything that has happened after the Incarnation points back to it. Again, Jesus is the center of the universe.

This also is why the answer to the question "Who is Jesus?" is a story. The Gospels are the answer to who Jesus is, and they are biographies. Jesus' whole life and death is the totality of divine Revelation because he is the Word of God itself, and so his whole life requires our attention.

The Gospel of John pays special attention to Jesus being the Word of God. John shows us how understanding Jesus as the Word ties together the eternal existence of the Son, his acts of creation and redemption, and the life of mankind:

> In the beginning was the Word, and the Word was with God, and the Word was God. He was in the beginning with God; all things were made through him, and without him was not anything made that was made. In him was life, and the life was the light of men. The light shines in the darkness, and the darkness has not overcome it. (John 1:1–5)

Jesus is the Word of the Father through whom all things came into being. To get an idea of what this means, think of how creative your own words are. We think in words. We form plans and ideas with words. We communicate within ourselves and to others through words. Human words are powerful: they can communicate ideas, they can help people, and they can hurt people. In a similar way, God communicates everything through his Word: Jesus Christ.

At the same time, humans don't just communicate with our words. We also communicate through our actions. We smile, we frown, we give our friends high-fives, and we hug our family members. In all these ways and countless more, we communicate who we are and what we feel, and often, our actions speak louder than words. It's powerful when a father tells his child that he loves him and even more powerful when he also gives the child a hug.

So too with God's Word! The language of God is powerful. It was powerful when he spoke through the prophets of the Old Testament, and it was even more powerful when the Son spoke as a man. But the Word of God, the total communication of God to us, includes all of Jesus Christ, his words and his deeds, and those deeds, just like the communication of a father to his child is both in his words and in his hug—speak powerfully. In Jesus, God doesn't just say who he is and how much he loves us; he shows us by becoming one of us, walking among us, healing the sick, raising the dead, and dying on a cross for us.

Throughout Salvation History, God had spoken to his people. No sooner did Adam and Eve commit the original sin than did God begin gathering together a people. He spoke to them and shepherded them, revealing bits of himself to them as they developed into a nation. This revelation of the Old Testament was also the Word of God. But, it was not his complete Word. His complete Word was the Incarnation of Jesus Christ.

Importantly, God's perfect communication of himself didn't go away when Jesus ascended into heaven. The Church is the Body of Christ, and the Word of God continues within her. The Word of God remains present to the world through his Church. We already saw how this was the case in Course 1, the Introduction to Fundamental Theology. The actual words of God persist in the Scriptures, in the Tradition in the liturgy of the Church. Likewise, the actions of God are preserved in the lives of the faithful, in the liturgical worship, and in the sacraments, especially the Eucharist, through which Christ's Body is really and truly present. Likewise, the Church continues Jesus' mission. His mission was a joint mission of the Son and the Holy Spirit, and that remains the case with the Church. The Church is the Mystical Body of Christ and the Holy Spirit guides it. By the power of the Holy Spirit, God's grace is poured out to the faithful through the sacraments. The mystery of the Church, like that of Christ, is a great mystery.

The Revelation of Jesus about God

ASSIGNED READING
CCC 234
CCC 237
CCC 255

God speaks his Word in order to communicate himself to us, and Jesus communicates God as a Blessed Trinity. Jesus reveals the "Communion of Love" which is the Persons of the Trinity: "the Father loves the Son, and has given all things into his hand" (John 3:35). Jesus also reveals and sends the Holy Spirit, saying: "And I will ask the Father, and he will give you another Counselor, to be with you forever" (John 14:16). Jesus actively communicates who God is. In our human limitations, however, we can only, ". . . see in a mirror dimly" (1 Cor 13:12). This is because God is essentially a mystery; he transcends human understanding.

The doctrine of the Trinity is the central mystery of Christian belief and is vitally important to a life of faith because when we love God and enter into a relationship with him, we encounter three divine persons. This can be confusing. Even the most brilliant thinkers have recognized the difficulty of this doctrine, and the Church has always recognized that the Trinity is a great mystery, so we shouldn't be discouraged by any difficulties we ourselves encounter as we try to wrap our minds around this truth.

It helps to know, though, that as we grow in our relationship with God, the difficulties of understanding the Trinity tend to fade away. That's not to say that the mystery is somehow solved, but rather that we become more comfortable with it—in fact, we come to love the mystery. This is similar to our relationships with other people. All of your human relationships need time and attention if you want them to deepen. You grow closer to a friend as you spend time with him and get to know him better, but there is always more to learn about him. Ylou may even discover that there are things about him that you are just never going to fully understand. This "mystery" about a person can be an obstacle to knowing him at first, but as a friendship deepens, it becomes something that you love, something that enriches your friendship because you know that it can always become deeper; there is no limit to how much more you can learn about your friend.

The same is true with God. We grow closer to him by spending time with him in prayer, by learning about him from the Scriptures and the teaching of the Church, and by loving him through following his commandments. As our relationship with God deepens, we come to understand more and more about who he is—a Trinity of three divine persons: Father, Son and Holy Spirit. But we never fully "understand" the Trinity. There is always more to the mystery than what we currently comprehend, so there is always more to learn and more opportunities for deepening our knowledge of God and our relationship with him.

Jesus' revelation of the nature of God was not meant to confuse us. Remember, we are made in God's image. He is totally beyond us, but he is not completely foreign to our understanding. This is why Jesus used common concepts to describe God. For example, Jesus tells us repeatedly that God is both his and our "Father" (Matt 6:9–15, 25–34; Luke 15:11–32; John 15:9), using filial (father/son) language to describe his relationship to God and his relationship to the Apostles. From what he says, we know not only that Jesus is the Son of God, but that we too are God's sons and daughters. This means that we are Jesus's brothers and sisters. This is helpful language to us because it is familiar. In fact, the family is one experience that virtually every person shares. It is also foundational for who we are as people.

Remember, when God created people, he created them male and female, and he told them to have children: we were created as a family. When God became a man, he entered into a human family—Mary and Joseph. When Jesus uses family imagery to explain who God is and to explain our relationship with God, he tells us something very real. God created us like him. That we are "like him" is called analogy. God is a Father by way of analogy to human fathers. By calling God our Father, we assert that God has the characteristics of a father: God is kind, loving, merciful, strong, etc., even if God is transcendent and beyond the grasp of total understanding.

SELECTED READING:
Congregation for the Doctrine of the Faith, Declaration on the Unicity and Salvific Universality of Jesus Christ and the Church *Dominus Iesus* (August 6, 2000), nos. 9–11

In contemporary theological reflection there often emerges an approach to Jesus of Nazareth that considers him a particular, finite, historical figure, who reveals the divine not in an exclusive way, but in a way complementary with other revelatory and salvific figures. The Infinite, the Absolute, the Ultimate Mystery of God would thus manifest itself to humanity in many ways and in many historical figures: Jesus of Nazareth would be one of these. More concretely, for some, Jesus would be one of the many faces which the Logos has assumed in the course of time to communicate with humanity in a salvific way.

Furthermore, to justify the universality of Christian salvation as well as the fact of religious pluralism, it has been proposed that there is an economy of the eternal Word that is valid also outside the Church and is unrelated to her, in addition to an economy of the incarnate Word. The first would have a greater universal value than the second, which is limited to Christians, though God's presence would be more full in the second.

These theses are in profound conflict with the Christian faith. The doctrine of faith must be firmly believed which proclaims that

Jesus of Nazareth, son of Mary, and he alone, is the Son and the Word of the Father. The Word, which "was in the beginning with God" (Jn 1:2) is the same as he who "became flesh" (Jn 1:14). In Jesus, "the Christ, the Son of the living God" (Mt 16:16), "the whole fullness of divinity dwells in bodily form" (Col 2:9). He is the "only begotten Son of the Father, who is in the bosom of the Father" (Jn 1:18), his "beloved Son, in whom we have redemption . . . In him the fullness of God was pleased to dwell, im, God was pleased to reconcile all things to himself, on earth and in the heavens, making peace by the blood of his Cross" (Col 1:13–14; 19–20).

Faithful to Sacred Scripture and refuting erroneous and reductive interpretations, the First Council of Nicaea solemnly defined its faith in: "Jesus Christ, the Son of God, the only begotten generated from the Father, that is, from the being of the Father, God from God, Light from Light, true God from true God, begotten, not made, one in being with the Father, through whom all things were made, those in heaven and those on earth. For us men and for our salvation, he came down and became incarnate, was made man, suffered, and rose again on the third day. He ascended to the heavens and shall come again to judge the living and the dead." Following the teachings of the Fathers of the Church, the Council of Chalcedon also professed: "the one and the same Son, our Lord Jesus Christ, the same perfect in divinity and perfect in humanity, the same truly God and truly man . . . , one in being with the Father according to the divinity and one in being with us according to the humanity . . . , begotten of the Father before the ages according to the divinity and, in these last days, for us and our salvation, of Mary, the Virgin Mother of God, according to the humanity."

For this reason, the Second Vatican Council states that Christ "the new Adam . . . 'image of the invisible God' (Col 1:15) is himself the perfect man who has restored that likeness to God in the children of Adam which had been disfigured since the first sin . . . As an innocent lamb he merited life for us by his blood which he freely shed. In him God reconciled us to himself and to one another, freeing us from the bondage of the devil and of sin, so that each one of us could say with the apostle: the Son of God 'loved me and gave himself up for me' (Gal 2:20)."

In this regard, John Paul II has explicitly declared: "To introduce any sort of separation between the Word and Jesus Christ is contrary to the Christian faith . . . Jesus is the Incarnate Word — a single and indivisible person . . . Christ is none other than Jesus of Nazareth; he is the Word of God made man for the salvation of all . . . In the process of discovering and appreciating the manifold gifts— especially the spiritual treasures—that God has bestowed on every people, we cannot separate those gifts from Jesus Christ, who is at the centre of God's plan of salvation."

It is likewise contrary to the Catholic faith to introduce a separation between the salvific action of the Word as such and that of the Word made man. With the incarnation, all the salvific actions of the Word of God are always done in unity with the human nature that he has assumed for the salvation of all people. The one subject which operates in the two natures, human and divine, is the single person of the Word.

Therefore, the theory which would attribute, after the incarnation as well, a salvific activity to the Logos as such in his divinity, exercised "in addition to" or "beyond" the humanity of Christ, is not compatible with the Catholic faith.

Similarly, the doctrine of faith regarding the unicity of the salvific economy willed by the One and Triune God must be firmly believed, at the source and centre of which is the mystery of the incarnation of the Word, mediator of divine grace on the level of creation and redemption (cf. Col 1:15–20), he who recapitulates all things (cf. Eph 1:10), he "whom God has made our wisdom, our righteousness, and sanctification and redemption" (1 Cor 1:30). In fact, the mystery of Christ has its own intrinsic unity, which extends from the eternal choice in God to the parousia: "he [the Father] chose us in Christ before the foundation of the world to be holy and blameless before him in love" (Eph 1:4); "In Christ we are heirs, having been destined according to the purpose of him who accomplishes all things according to his counsel and will" (Eph 1:11); "For those whom he foreknew he also predestined to be conformed to the image of his Son, in order that he might be the firstborn among many brothers; those whom he predestined he also called; and those whom he called he also justified; and those whom he justified he also glorified" (Rom 8:29–30).

The Church's Magisterium, faithful to divine revelation, reasserts that Jesus Christ is the mediator and the universal redeemer: "The Word of God, through whom all things were made, was made flesh, so that as perfect man he could save all men and sum up all things in himself. The Lord . . . is he whom the Father raised from the dead, exalted and placed at his right hand, constituting him judge of the living and the dead." This salvific mediation implies also the unicity of the redemptive sacrifice of Christ, eternal high priest (cf. Heb 6:20; 9:11; 10:12–14).

QUESTIONS FOR REVIEW

1. How many natures did Jesus have?
2. Is Jesus a human person, a divine person, or both?
3. Who is the Word of God?
4. How did Jesus communicate to us?
5. What is the most fundamental and mysterious truth about God that we learned from Jesus?

QUESTIONS FOR DISCUSSION

1. Name two actions of yours today that have revealed something about who you are.
2. Think of what you know about Jesus' life and name one action of his that stands out. What does that tell you about him, and in turn, about God?
3. What, besides the Holy Trinity, is one of life's mysteries—something you feel like you can never fully understand? When you run up against a mystery, do you want to know more about it? If so, why? Do you feel this way about the mysteries of faith? Why or why not?

Chapter 2

THE THREE DIVINE PERSONS
OF THE TRINITY

ASSIGNED READING
John 3:1–21
John 10:22–30
John 14:8–11
John 15:18–27
John 17:20–26
Mark 12:28–34
CCC 232–248

The First Person of the Trinity:
God the Father

Jesus reveals God as a loving and merciful Father. The Church recognizes
God to be Father in a number of ways:

The Father as the Source of All That Is

This is the first biblical image of God: "In the beginning God created the
heavens and the earth" (Gen 1:1). Similarly, the whole divine economy
shows God's efforts to renew his creation, making it possible for it to

share in his divine life (see 2 Pet 1:3–5). Like our human fathers and mothers, God is the source of our life. This is important to understand, for it reminds us that we are contingent beings. We did not create ourselves nor our world, and we owe our existence to God.

Father and Son

St. John's Gospel begins, "In the beginning was the Word, and the Word was with God, and the Word was God" (John 1:1). This tells us that Jesus is eternally in relation to the Father. We can only call someone a father if they have a son or daughter, and we can only call someone a son if they have a father. This is what we mean when we say that "father" and "son" are relational terms: their definitions depend on each other. The Father in the Trinity, therefore, is a Father because the Son is also in the Trinity. They are in constant relation to each other. The Catechism states:

> Jesus revealed that God is Father in an unheard-of sense: he is Father not only in being Creator; he is eternally Father in relation to his only Son, who is eternally Son only in relation to his Father: "No one knows the Son except the Father, and no one knows the Father except the Son and any one to whom the Son chooses to reveal him" [*Mt* 11:27]. (CCC 240)

God Is Father of All the Baptized

St. Paul says in the Letter to the Romans,

> When we cry, "Abba! Father!" it is the Spirit himself bearing witness with our spirit that we are children of God, and if children, then heirs, heirs of God and fellow heirs with Christ, provided we suffer with him in order that we may also be glorified with him." (Rom 8:15–17)

Through Baptism, we become the adopted brothers of Jesus Christ and the adopted sons and daughters of the Father. We are heirs to the kingdom of God, and as Jesus called God "Abba" (see Mark 14:36), so we too call God "Abba." This means that we participate in the relationship between God the Father and God the Son. In a sense, we become a part of the family of the Trinity. This is why, when Jesus taught us to pray, he told us to refer to God as "Our Father" (Matt 6:9).

God Is Father of All and Cares for All

In 1 Timothy 2:3–4, St. Paul writes that God "desires all men to be saved and to come to the knowledge of the truth." This reminds us that God watches over and cares for all. God is the Father of all people, even if they don't accept their sonship. Like the father in the parable of the prodigal son (Luke 15:11–32), God is a forgiving and loving Father who patiently waits for us to accept his invitation to come home. He extends this invitation to everyone—to those who have fallen away from the faith and to those who have not yet heard the Gospel. That he sent his Son, Jesus Christ, to die for the sins of the whole world is proof that God is the Father of everyone.

The Second Person of the Trinity: God the Son

Jesus Christ Is True God, Consubstantial with the Father

The Nicene Creed states,

> I believe in one Lord Jesus Christ, the Only Begotten Son of God, born of the Father before all ages. God from God, Light from Light, true God from true God, begotten, not made, consubstantial with the Father.

Every Sunday, at Mass, we say those words. We say that the three Persons of the Trinity are consubstantial with each other. But what does "consubstantial" mean? The answer comes from Greek philosophy. In the Greek philosophical tradition, the term "substance" meant what a thing is at its deepest level of being. So for example, we human beings have humanity at the core of our being. It's what defines us. You can change your hair color or eye color, your home or your job, but no matter what you change about yourself, you will still have your humanity, and so you will remain a human person. A thing's substance is the unchangeable essence of what that thing is. Our substance is humanity. God's substance is divinity.

Note: the Persons of the Trinity each have divinity fully. The Father is God, the Son is God, and the Spirit is God. The Father is not 33.33 percent God or 50 percent God or any part or percentage of God. Rather, the Father is 100 percent God, the Son is 100 percent God, and the Spirit is 100 percent God. Each possesses full divinity, like you possess full humanity. This is what it means to be consubstantial—each possesses the same substance. Unlike humanity, however, the essence of divinity is only one. As humans, we are part of humanity; we are one member of the community of human beings. This isn't the case with divinity. The Father, Son, and Holy Spirit aren't part of a community of gods. There can't be multiple gods that have true divinity. Therefore, the Trinity is not three gods. God is One—one God in three individual, consubstantial Persons.

This is a hard concept and many helpful analogies have been offered by theologians. The most obvious is the family. The Trinity is like a family in that a family is a single thing made up of multiple persons. But that analogy only goes so far. Like all analogies, it can helpful but it can't convey the fullness of the mystery. The unity of divinity is different from any type of unity that can be experienced by people.

Jesus Christ Is the Only Begotten Son of God, Born of the Father before All Ages

The Holy Trinity does not have a personal history, with a beginning or a middle or an end. This is because the Trinity exists outside of time. In fact, time is a part of his creation. God made time. We believe that the Son is begotten, or born from, the Father, but this isn't something that happened at some point in time. There never was a time before the Son was born from the Father. Rather, the Son exists in a relationship of begottenness with the Father. This is a really difficult idea, but essentially the Son is, in a sense, constantly being "begotten" or born of the Father. Remember there is not "before" or "after" with God. This is why it is not the case that the Father created the Son. Rather, they have from all eternity been together. However, when the eternal Son became incarnate, when he became a man, he entered into time. He entered into our history.

Jesus Is the New Adam / the New Man

Together, let's read Genesis 3, the story of original sin, and see how Adam failed.

> Now the serpent was more subtle than any other wild creature that the Lord God had made. He said to the woman, "Did God say, 'You shall not eat of any tree of the garden'?" And the woman said to the serpent, "We may eat of the fruit of the trees of the garden; but God said, 'You shall not eat of the fruit of the tree which is in the midst of the garden, neither shall you touch it, lest you die.'" But the serpent said to the woman, "You will not die. For God knows that when you eat of it your eyes will be opened, and you will be like God, knowing good and evil." So when the woman saw that the tree was good for food, and that it was a delight to the eyes, and that the tree was to be desired to make one wise, she took of its fruit and ate; and she also gave some to her husband, and he ate. Then the eyes of both were opened, and they knew that they were naked; and they sewed fig leaves together and made themselves aprons. And they heard the sound of the Lord God walking in the garden in the cool of the day, and the man and his wife hid themselves from the presence of the Lord God among the trees of the garden. But the Lord God called to the man, and said to him, "Where are you?" And he said, "I heard the sound of thee in the garden, and I was afraid, because I was naked; and I hid myself." He said, "Who told you

that you were naked? Have you eaten of the tree of which I commanded you not to eat?" The man said, "The woman whom you gave to be with me, she gave me fruit of the tree, and I ate." Then the LORD God said to the woman, "What is this that you have done?" The woman said, "The serpent beguiled me, and I ate." The LORD God said to the serpent,

> "Because you have done this,
>> cursed are you above all cattle,
>> and above all wild animals;
> upon your belly you shall go,
>> and dust you shall eat
>> all the days of your life.
> I will put enmity between you and the woman,
>> and between your seed and her seed;
> he shall bruise your head,
>> and you shall bruise his heel."
> To the woman he said,
> "I will greatly multiply your pain in childbearing;
>> in pain you shall bring forth children,
> yet your desire shall be for your husband,
>> and he shall rule over you."
> And to Adam he said,
> "Because you have listened to the voice of your wife,
>> and have eaten of the tree
> of which I commanded you,
>> 'You shall not eat of it,'
> cursed is the ground because of you;
>> in toil you shall eat of it all the days of your life;
> thorns and thistles it shall bring forth to you;
>> and you shall eat the plants of the field.
> In the sweat of your face
>> you shall eat bread
> till you return to the ground,
>> for out of it you were taken;

you are dust,
and to dust you shall return."

The man called his wife's name Eve, because she was the mother of all living. And the LORD God made for Adam and for his wife garments of skins, and clothed them. Then the LORD God said, "Behold, the man has become like one of us, knowing good and evil; and now, lest he put forth his hand and take also of the tree of life, and eat, and live for ever"—therefore the LORD God sent him forth from the garden of Eden, to till the ground from which he was taken. He drove out the man; and at the east of the garden of Eden he placed the cherubim, and a flaming sword which turned every way, to guard the way to the tree of life.

The Hebrew word *adam* means "man," which is also a term used for all humanity. So, the story of the fall of Adam is the story of the fall of humanity itself. This means when the Church calls Jesus the new Adam, it's saying that Jesus is a new type of mankind. As Adam damaged all mankind, so Jesus repairs all mankind. St. Paul writes: "For as by one man's disobedience many were made sinners, so by one man's obedience many will be made righteous" (Rom 5:19–20), and "For as by a man came death, by a man has come also the resurrection of the dead" (1 Cor 15:21–22).

Jesus is conceived by the Holy Spirit in the Virgin Mary's womb because he is the New Adam, who inaugurates the new creation: "The first man was from the earth, a man of dust; the second man is from heaven" [*1 Cor* 15:45, 47]. From his conception, Christ's humanity is filled with the Holy Spirit, for God "gives him the Spirit without measure" [*Jn* 3:34]. From "his fullness" as the head of redeemed humanity "we have all received, grace upon grace" [*Jn* 1:16; cf. *Col* 1:18]. (CCC 504)

Jesus is the new Adam because Jesus is the perfect man. In his humanity, Jesus is what and who the first man was made to be. He is what and who we are made to be. Jesus shows us what it looks like to be a perfect human being. But even more than that, as our Savior, Jesus makes it possible through grace for us to join him in this perfection. Through him we are made into a "new creation."

Jesus as Savior and Redeemer

Jesus' whole life was dedicated to bringing us into communion with God. He is our Redeemer, the one who bought us back from sin, paying the price for us to become a new creation with the offering of his life. As our Redeemer, Jesus brings about not simply our own personal salvation, but also the recapitulation of the entire world (CCC 517–518).

"Recapitulation" literally means "to restore headship," which is to say that Jesus came to restore God as the head of creation. When Adam and Eve sinned, they cast God aside. Jesus, through his Crucifixion, Resurrection, and Ascension, places God squarely at the center of creation once again. St. Paul states in Colossians 1:18–20:

> He is the head of the body, the church; he is the beginning, the firstborn from the dead, so that he might come to have first place in everything. For in him all the fullness of God was pleased to dwell, and through him God was pleased to reconcile to himself all things, whether on earth or in heaven, by making peace through the blood of his cross.

Jesus Christ, being both God and man, bridged the gap that had opened up between heaven and earth. When we are united with Jesus, we participate in this "bridging of the gap." The faithful—those united with Jesus and with each other—make up the Body of Christ, which is the Church. When we are a part of the Body of Christ, the gap between heaven and earth is bridged for us because Christ is that bridge. This is the salvation that our Savior Christ brought to us. The Church, then, is the continuation of Christ's mission on earth. It is through his Church that the redemptive mission of the Holy Spirit continues.

The Third Person of the Trinity: The Holy Spirit, "The Lord, the Giver of Life"

The Nicene Creed describes the Holy Spirit as one "who proceeds from the Father and the Son," but that doesn't tell us much. In many ways, the Holy Spirit is perhaps the hardest Person of the Trinity for us to understand. Through analogy, we have some understanding of the Father and the Son, but the Holy Spirit often seems veiled or hidden.

Nevertheless, while the Trinity is a great mystery, and human understanding is never going to get it just right, one of the most helpful descriptions the Church gives us is that the Holy Spirit is the eternal love shared between the Father and Son. This, in part, is because love is fruitful. One of the things that love does is create. We see this, for example, in the family. When a man and a women love each other, their love bears fruit in the form of a new person, a child. By analogy, we can see that the love shared between the Father and the Son is also fruitful, with the divine person of the Holy Spirit proceeding from that love. Since the love between the Father and the Son is eternal (it has no beginning, no before and after), the Holy Spirit eternally proceeds from them. There never was a time before the Holy Spirit. God is from all eternity all three persons.

Jesus revealed to us the existence of the Holy Spirit, as he revealed to us the existence of himself as the Son. The Holy Spirit might be understood as the Person of the Trinity who acts directly in history. The Holy Spirit goes "out" from the Father and the Son. It is through the Holy Spirit that God's grace, through which our sanctification is made possible, is brought to the world. This work of sanctification is carried out through the mission of the Church. So, in a sense, the Holy Spirit is the "soul" of the Church; he is the reality that makes the Church alive and more than just a society of people.

> The mission of Christ and the Holy Spirit is brought to completion in the Church, which is the Body of Christ and the Temple of the Holy Spirit. This joint mission henceforth brings Christ's faithful to share in his communion with the Father in the Holy Spirit. The Spirit *prepares* men and goes out to them with his

grace, in order to draw them to Christ. The Spirit *manifests* the risen Lord to them, recalls his word to them and opens their minds to the understanding of his Death and Resurrection. He *makes present* the mystery of Christ, supremely in the Eucharist, in order to reconcile them, to *bring them into communion* with God, that they may "bear much fruit" [*Jn* 15:8, 16]. (CCC 737)

The Holy Spirit is active not only in the life of the Church as a whole, but also in the life of each individual Christian. The Church has traditionally identified seven gifts that the Holy Spirit gives to the baptized. These are: wisdom, understanding, counsel, fortitude, knowledge, piety, and fear of the Lord. These gifts are the result of the grace that the Holy Spirit offers us. Like all grace, though, we need to cooperate with it. The Holy Spirit offers us wonderful gifts, but we need to accept them.

When we do, we enjoy the "fruits of the Holy Spirit." The Church has traditionally identified twelve fruits of the Holy Spirit: charity, joy, peace, patience, kindness, goodness, generosity, gentleness, faithfulness, modesty, self-control, and chastity (Gal 5:22–23). We can see in the gifts and fruits of the Holy Spirit the whole moral life of mankind. Jesus possesses all the gifts and fruits perfectly, and we are both called and empowered to follow his example. This is the work of the Holy Spirit.

The Development of Trinitarian Theology

Doctrine and Dogma

The existence of the Trinity is a doctrine or dogma of the Catholic Church. Doctrines and dogmas make up the core of our beliefs. They articulate what we have learned to be true about God. Unfortunately, many today react negatively to the words "doctrine" or "dogma." The mainstream culture uses the words "doctrinaire" or "dogmatic" as synonyms for "boring," "uncreative," and even "narrow-minded" or "tyrannical." In that, however, they couldn't be more wrong. Consider the great English author G.K. Chesterton's response:

Some people do not like the word "dogma." Fortunately they are free, and there is an alternative for them. There are two things, and two things only, for the human mind, a dogma and a prejudice. The Middle Ages were a rational epoch, an age of doctrine. Our age is, at its best, a poetical epoch, an age of prejudice. A doctrine is a definite point; a prejudice is a direction. That an ox may be eaten, while a man should not be eaten, is a doctrine. That as little as possible of anything should be eaten is a prejudice; which is also sometimes called an ideal. Now a direction is always far more fantastic than a plan. I would rather have the most archaic map of the road to Brighton than a general recommendation to turn to the left. Straight lines that are not parallel must meet at last; but curves may recoil forever. A pair of lovers might walk along the frontier of France and Germany, one on the one side and one on the other, so long as they were not vaguely told to keep away from each other. And this is a strictly true parable of the effect of our modern vagueness in losing and separating men as in a mist.[1]

Man can hardly be defined, after the fashion of Carlyle, as an animal who makes tools; ants and beavers and many other animals make tools, in the sense that they make an apparatus. Man can be defined as an animal that makes dogmas. As he piles doctrine on doctrine and conclusion on conclusion in the formation of some tremendous scheme of philosophy and religion, he is, in the only legitimate sense of which the expression is capable, becoming more and more human. When he drops one doctrine after another in a refined skepticism, when he declines to tie himself to a system, when he says that he has outgrown definitions, when he says that he disbelieves in finality, when, in his own imagination, he sits as God, holding no form of creed but contemplating all, then he is by that very process sinking

---

[1] Gilbert K. Chesterton, *What's Wrong with the World* (New York: Dodd, Mead and Company, 1912), 21.

slowly backwards into the vagueness of the vagrant animals and the unconsciousness of the grass. Trees have no dogmas. Turnips are singularly broad-minded.[2]

The truth is, doctrines and dogmas can be very good, especially those that teach us about the nature of God. They help us know with whom we are invited to have a relationship, and they help us recognize ideas that aren't compatible with who we know God to be. With this recognition, one can respectfully engage with people who hold other ideas. Because we know where we stand, we become capable of tolerating with charity those who stand somewhere else. We also become capable of arguing with them without feeling threatened or getting angry. It's no coincidence that those who are the most adverse to "dogma" are often those who get the most angry when they encounter someone who disagrees with them.

As we have seen, the doctrine of the Trinity is a particularly difficult dogma to understand. It is a great and beautiful mystery that no one would devise on their own. We maintain it, even though it's so mysterious, precisely because we have, through our relationship with God, come to know it as true. This didn't happen overnight, though. It actually took several centuries, because the Church had to consider the teachings of Jesus in Scripture and Tradition, and the faithful had to worship and pray. In the process of doing so the Church entered more deeply into a relationship with God and so learned more and more about him.

In theology, this process is called the "development of doctrine." Through the development of doctrine, the Church does not create new truths. Rather, it articulates in an ever-clearer way what the faithful always knew at some level to be true about God. The first Christians knew that Jesus was the Son of God, whom he referred to as Father. They also knew that Jesus promised that the Holy Spirit would come, and they knew that the God of Israel was one. Above all, they knew that Jesus himself told the Apostles to baptize "in the name of the Father and of the Son and of the Holy Spirit" (Matt 28:19). Eventually all these points of

---

2   Gilbert K. Chesterton, *Heretics* (New York: John Lane Company, 1919), 286.

knowledge came together to form the doctrine of the Trinity as we know it today.

Heresies and Ecumenical Councils

Again, though, that process took time. In the early centuries of Christianity, there was actually a great deal of disagreement about the three Persons—Father, Son, and Holy Spirit—and many different theories were proposed. As the Church's magisterium encountered these theories, it sorted out the true ones from the false ones. The ones deemed true were those consistent both with the facts of Scripture and Tradition and with the Church's experience of relationship with God. The ones deemed false were those inconsistent with these things.

A false belief about God is called a heresy. Right beliefs are called orthodoxy. In many ways, orthodox beliefs concerning Jesus and the Trinity have been defined because the Church has had to point out why various theories were, in fact, heresies. This is to say that heresies, in a sense, helped the Church more fully and accurately articulate what was really true about God.

One of the first heresies the Church encountered was Gnosticism. Gnosticism was "dualist," meaning that the Gnostics believed the physical world was evil and corrupt and the spiritual world was perfect. They believed that the two worlds did not mix and each had their own god—the material god was bad and the spiritual god was good. Jesus, they claimed, was from the good god. This meant, of course, that he could not have really had a human body because bodies were evil. Gnostics, therefore, denied that Jesus was really a human. But from the time of the New Testament the Church insisted that Jesus really did come "in the flesh" (1 John 4:2–3; 2 John 7).

After Gnosticism came Arianism. Arianism was founded by a man named Arius of Alexandria (c. AD 260–336). Arius couldn't accept that Jesus was both God and man. He believed this to be a paradox and so asserted that Jesus wasn't really God, but rather God's most important and perfect creation. Arianism was attractive to many because it seemed to solve a mystery: how could Jesus be both God and man? However, at the First Council of Nicaea in AD 325, the Church declared Arianism a heresy. The council then drafted the Nicene Creed in defense of the orthodox belief in the divinity of Christ. It asserted that the Son was consubstantial with the Father.

Unfortunately, the Council of Nicaea didn't stop Arianism, which continued to spread. Moreover, around the same time, a new heresy sprang up: Macedonianism. Macedonianism asserted that while the Son was truly God, along with the Father, the Holy Spirit was not. In response, the Church called the First Council of Constantinople (AD 381). This Council condemned both Arianism and Macedonianism as heresies and issued a revised creed, the Nicene-Constantinopolitan Creed. This creed is basically the same as that which we recite at Mass even to this day. Among other additions, the Council added the section that starts "And in the Holy Spirit, the Lord the giver of life . . ."

While the Council of Constantinople settled many of the issues surrounding the Trinity, more disputes arose, most of these concerning the Incarnation of the Son. How, people asked, could Jesus be both God and man? Like the Trinity, this is a great mystery, and people wanted to find a solution to it; they wanted to bring it down to a level they could understand. Nestorianism was one attempt. It held that within Jesus there were actually two distinct persons—the divine Son of God and the human Jesus. This was really a denial of the Incarnation itself because it means that, in Jesus, the Son of God did not so much become a man as live alongside a man. The Nestorians, therefore, denied that Mary was the Mother of God. Rather, they claimed, she was only the mother of the human Jesus. Accordingly, in AD 431, the Council of Ephesus was called to combat Nestorianism. The bishops who gathered there confirmed the teaching that Jesus is one Person—the divine Son of God—who assumed a human nature. The Council also confirmed the title *Theotokos,* "Mother of God," for the Blessed Mother. Mary has been honored with this title ever since.

Even after all these councils, it remained somewhat unclear how, in the one Person of Christ, the divine and human were related. One theory, called Monophysitism, maintained that Jesus had one nature that was both fully divine and fully human. The problem was that this theory tended to emphasize the divine at the expense of the human, so it seemed like Jesus' human nature was absorbed into the divine. This view was condemned at the Council of Chalcedon (AD 451). That Council asserted that in Christ, there are two natures—the divine nature and a full human nature—united in the one person of the Son of God:

> Therefore, following the holy fathers, we all teach that with one accord we confess one and the same Son, our Lord Jesus Christ, the same perfect in human nature, truly God and the same with a rational soul and a body truly man, consubstantial with the Father according to divinity, and consubstantial with us according to human nature, like unto us in all things except sin, [cf. Heb. 4:15]; indeed born of the Father before the ages according to divine nature, but in the last days the same born of the virgin Mary, Mother of God, according to human nature; for us and for our deliverance, one and the same Christ only begotten Son, our Lord, acknowledged in two natures, without mingling, without change, indivisibly, undividedly, the distinction of the natures nowhere removed on account of the union but rather the peculiarity of each nature being kept, and uniting in one person and substance, not divided or separated into two persons, but one and the same Son only begotten God Word, Lord Jesus Christ, just as from the beginning the prophets taught about Him and the Lord Jesus Himself taught us, and the creed of our fathers has handed down to us. (DS 301–302)

Together, over the course of 400 years, these ecumenical councils articulated the dogmas of the Trinity and Incarnation, the two central beliefs of Christianity. Through them, we came to more fully understand that God is three Persons with one divine nature, and one of these Persons, the Son, became truly man, uniting to himself a full human nature; he was like us in all things except sin. Any teaching that challenges this doctrine is not Catholic teaching.

The development of doctrine, however, is not over. For example, in the twentieth century, in the face of the "sexual revolution" and the breakdown of marriage, significant developments have been made concerning human sexuality and the role of the family in the life of the Church, especially through the work of Pope St. John Paul II. Far from being narrow-minded or tyrannical, the Church's doctrine is responsive to the needs of the times. This isn't to say that Church doctrine changes. It doesn't. Rather, the Holy Spirit works through the magisterium to respond to a real need for deeper understanding. Heresies are in no way a thing of the past. Even today, people challenge the Church's doctrine. Some see Jesus as just a good man or a powerful moral teacher, and deny his divinity. Others (often associated with the "New Age" movement) argue that we are all God or that the whole world is actually God. The Church continues to respond to these errors by presenting again and again the truth of Jesus Christ as handed on to the Apostles and through them to the bishops.

SELECTED READING:
Saint Augustine, *On the Trinity*, bk. 1, chap. 6

They who have said that our Lord Jesus Christ is not God, or not very God, or not with the Father the One and only God, or not truly immortal because changeable, are proved wrong by the most plain and unanimous voice of divine testimonies; as, for instance, "In the beginning was the Word, and the Word was with God, and the Word was God." For it is plain that we are to take the Word of God to be the only Son of God, of whom it is afterwards said, "And the Word was made flesh, and dwelt among us," on account of that birth of His incarnation, which was wrought in time of the Virgin. But herein is declared, not only that He is God, but also that He is of the same substance with the Father; because, after saying, "And the Word was God," it is said also, "The same was in the beginning with God: all things were made by Him, and without Him was not anything made." Not simply all things; but only all things that were made, that is; the whole creature. From which it appears clearly, that He Himself was not made, by whom all things were made. And if He was not made, then He is not a creature; but if He is not a creature, then He is of the same substance with the Father. For all substance that is not God is creature; and all that is not creature is God. And if the Son is not of the same substance with the Father, then He is a substance that was made: and if He is a substance that was made, then all things were not made by Him; but "all things were made by Him," therefore He is of one and the same substance with the Father. And so He is not only God, but also very God. And the same John most expressly affirms this in his epistle: "For we know that the Son of God has come, and has given us an understanding, that we may know the true God, and that we may be in His true Son Jesus Christ. This is the true God, and eternal life."

Hence also it follows by consequence, that the Apostle Paul did not say, "Who alone has immortality," of the Father merely; but of the One and only God, which is the Trinity itself. For that which is itself eternal life is not mortal according to any changeableness; and hence the Son of God, because "He is Eternal Life," is also Himself understood with the Father, where it is said, "Who only has immortality." For we, too, are made partakers of this eternal life, and become, in our own measure, immortal. But the eternal life itself, of which we are made partakers, is one thing; we ourselves, who, by partaking of it, shall live eternally, are another. For if He had said, "Whom in His own time the Father will show, who is the blessed and only Potentate, the King of kings, and Lord of lords; who only has immortality;" not even so would it be necessarily understood that the Son is excluded. For neither has the Son separated the Father from Himself, because He Himself, speaking elsewhere with the voice of wisdom (for He Himself is the Wisdom of God), says, "I alone compassed the circuit of heaven." And therefore so much the more is it not necessary that the words, "Who has immortality," should be understood of the Father alone, omitting the Son; when they are said thus: "That you keep this commandment without spot, unrebukeable, until the appearing of our Lord Jesus Christ: whom in His own time He will show, who is the blessed and only Potentate, the King of kings, and Lord of lords; who only has immortality, dwelling in the light which no man

71

can approach unto; whom no man has seen, nor can see: to whom be honor and power everlasting. Amen." In which words neither is the Father specially named, nor the Son, nor the Holy Spirit; but the blessed and only Potentate, the King of kings, and Lord of lords; that is, the One and only and true God, the Trinity itself.

But perhaps what follows may interfere with this meaning; because it is said, "Whom no man has seen, nor can see:" although this may also be taken as belonging to Christ according to His divinity, which the Jews did not see, who yet saw and crucified Him in the flesh; whereas His divinity can in no way be seen by human sight, but is seen with that sight with which they who see are no longer men, but beyond men. Rightly, therefore, is God Himself, the Trinity, understood to be the "blessed and only Potentate," who "shows the coming of our Lord Jesus Christ in His own time." For the words, "Who only has immortality," are said in the same way as it is said, "Who only does wondrous things." And I should be glad to know of whom they take these words to be said. If only of the Father, how then is that true which the Son Himself says, "For whatever things the Father does, these also does the Son likewise?" Is there any, among wonderful works, more wonderful than to raise up and quicken the dead? Yet the same Son says, "As the Father raises up the dead, and quickens them, even so the Son quickens whom He will." How, then, does the Father alone do wondrous things, when these words allow us to understand neither the Father only, nor the Son only, but assuredly the one only true God, that is, the Father, and the Son, and the Holy Spirit?

Also, when the same apostle says, "But to us there is but one God, the Father, of whom are all things, and we in Him; and one Lord Jesus Christ, by whom are all things, and we by Him," who can doubt that he speaks of all things which are created; as does John, when he says, "All things were made by Him"? I ask, therefore, of whom he speaks in another place: "For of Him, and through Him, and in Him, are all things: to whom be glory forever. Amen." For if of the Father, and the Son, and the Holy Spirit, so as to assign each clause severally to each person: of Him, that is to say, of the Father;

through Him, that is to say, through the Son; in Him, that is to say, in the Holy Spirit—it is manifest that the Father, and the Son, and the Holy Spirit is one God, inasmuch as the words continue in the singular number, "To whom be glory forever." For at the beginning of the passage he does not say, "O the depth of the riches both of the wisdom and knowledge of the Father, or of the Son, or of the Holy Spirit, but of the wisdom and knowledge of God! How unsearchable are His judgments, and His ways past finding out! For who has known the mind of the Lord? Or who has been His counselor? Or who has first given to Him and it shall be recompensed unto him again? For of Him, and through Him, and in Him, are all things: to whom be glory forever. Amen." But if they will have this to be understood only of the Father, then in what way are all things by the Father, as is said here; and all things by the Son, as where it is said to the Corinthians, "And one Lord Jesus Christ, by whom are all things," and as in the Gospel of John, "All things were made by Him?" For if some things were made by the Father, and some by the Son, then all things were not made by the Father, nor all things by the Son; but if all things were made by the Father, and all things by the Son, then the same things were made by the Father and by the Son. The Son, therefore, is equal with the Father, and the working of the Father and the Son is indivisible. Because if the Father made even the Son, whom certainly the Son Himself did not make, then all things were not made by the Son; but all things were made by the Son: therefore He Himself was not made, that with the Father He might make all things that were made. And the apostle has not refrained from using the very word itself, but has said most expressly, "Who, being in the form of God, thought it not robbery to be equal with God;" using here the name of God specially of the Father; as elsewhere, "But the head of Christ is God."

Similar evidence has been collected also concerning the Holy Spirit, of which those who have discussed the subject before ourselves have most fully availed themselves, that He too is God, and not a creature. But if not a creature, then not only God (for men likewise are called gods), but also very God; and therefore absolutely equal with the Father and the Son, and in the unity of the Trinity consubstantial and co-eternal. But that the Holy Spirit is not a creature is made quite plain by that passage above all others, where we are commanded not to serve the creature, but the Creator; not in the sense in which we are commanded to "serve" one another by love . . . but in that in which God alone is served . . . Now if we are forbidden to serve the creature with such a service, seeing that it is written, "You shall worship the Lord your God, and Him only shall you serve" (and hence, too, the apostle repudiates those who worship and serve the creature more than the Creator), then assuredly the Holy Spirit is not a creature, to whom such a service is paid by all the saints; as says the apostle, "For we are the circumcision, which serve the Spirit of God," . . . For even most Latin copies also have it thus, "We who serve the Spirit of God;" but all Greek ones, or almost all, have it so. Although in some Latin copies we find, not "We worship the Spirit of God," but, "We worship God in the Spirit." But let those who err in this case, and refuse to give up to the more weighty authority, tell us whether they find this text also varied in the manuscripts: "Do you not know that your body is the temple of the Holy Ghost, which is in you, which you have of God?" Yet what can be more senseless or more profane, than that any one should dare to say that the members of Christ are the temple of one who, in their opinion, is a creature inferior to Christ? For the apostle says in another place, "Your bodies are members of Christ." But if the members of Christ are also the temple of the Holy Spirit, then the Holy Spirit is not a creature; because we must needs owe to Him, of whom our body is the temple, that service wherewith God only is to be served, which in Greek is called λατρεία. And accordingly the apostle says, "Therefore glorify God in your body."

QUESTIONS FOR REVIEW

1. Which Person of the Holy Trinity is associated with the mission of creation?
2. Which Person of the Holy Trinity is associated with mission of redemption?
3. Which Person of the Holy Trinity is associated with the work of sanctification?
4. Name one early heresy about Jesus. What did the heresy claim? Why was it wrong?
5. How have heresies helped in the process of the development of doctrine?

QUESTIONS FOR DISCUSSION

1. Do you struggle to see God as Father? Why or why not?
2. Jesus is our redeemer. He is also our brother. How do you relate to Jesus as a brother?
3. What fruits of the Holy Spirit do you see in your life? Which fruits are missing? Why do you think that might be?

Chapter 3

Mary, the Blessed Mother

ASSIGNED READING
Genesis 3:8–20
John 19:25–27
Galatians 4:1–5
Revelation 12
CCC 484–495

As we have already seen, the Church venerates Mary under the title *Theotokos*, the Mother of God. This devotion to Mary has always been rooted in devotion to Jesus himself. If Jesus was truly man and truly God in one person, and Mary was the mother of that person, then it is absolutely right to say that Mary is the Mother of God.

In addition to calling Mary the Mother of God, the Church also describes her as the New Eve. Eve, remember, said no to God in the garden of Eden when she disobeyed him, and through this disobedience, death entered the world. Mary, on the other hand, said yes to God. At the Annunciation, Mary said to the Angel Gabriel, "Behold, I am the handmaid of the Lord; let it be done to me according to your word" (Luke 1:38). Through this yes, the Savior of the human race entered the world, and death was defeated. This is why Mary is the New Eve, the perfect woman through whom the New Adam, Jesus, the perfect man, entered the world. Pope St. John Paul II explained it this way:

This fiat of Mary—"let it be to me"—was decisive, on the human level, for the accomplishment of the divine mystery. There is a complete harmony with the words of the Son, who, according to the Letter to the Hebrews, says to the Father as he comes into the world: "Sacrifices and offering you have not desired, but a body you have prepared for me. . . . Lo, I have come to do your will, O God" (Heb. 10:5–7). The mystery of the Incarnation was accomplished when Mary uttered her fiat: "Let it be to me according to your word," which made possible, as far as it depended upon her in the divine plan, the granting of her Son's desire.[1]

The Immaculate Conception of Mary

At the Annunciation, the angel referred to Mary as "full of grace." The Church connects this greeting to her understanding that through grace, Mary was preserved from all sin from the moment of her conception, even original sin. This is the Catholic dogma of the Immaculate Conception. This might seem like a strange or difficult dogma, and most Protestant Christians today deny it. Nevertheless, many reasons exist that can help us make sense of the Immaculate Conception and understand it as a necessary development of the dogma of the Incarnation.

The first reason goes back to Mary's role as the New Eve. Eve, of course, was created without original sin. She made her choice of disobedience while in the state of original grace (CCC 375) and so her choice was totally free. Mary, the New Eve, also needed to make a free choice. Her yes needed to be totally free. Her freedom from sin made that possible.

Second, Scripture testifies that nothing unclean or unholy can touch God. Consider the story of Nadab and Abihu (Lev 10:1–2), who offered unworthy incense in the Temple and were consumed by fire. Look also at the attention to detail in which the Tabernacle was constructed (Exod

---

[1] John Paul II, Encyclical Letter on the Blessed Virgin Mary in the Life of the Pilgrim Church *Redemptoris Mater* (March 25, 1987), §13.

35–40) and all the laws that governed the activity in the Tabernacle (Num 15). This, of course, was a man-made dwelling for God, constructed of cloth and wood, and so it could never really be perfect. Mary, however, was the dwelling place that God made for himself, and God can make something perfect. Mary is God's most perfect creation because she was made to be God's dwelling place and mother.

This raises a third point. In the Ten Commandments, God ordered men to honor their mothers and fathers. The Ten Commandments aren't arbitrary. They are part of God's rules for living a righteous life—a life that is pleasing to him. Jesus Christ was God, but he was also a perfectly righteous man. How much more could Jesus have honored his own mother than by preserving her from all defects? God created and maintains his mother in perfect communion with him as the perfect woman because he is the perfect Son who honors his mother perfectly.

The Assumption of Mary into Heaven

The Church teaches that when Mary reached the end of her life, she was raised, body and soul, to heaven. Her body did not see decay on Earth but was raised to glory with her Son, who after the resurrection also has a glorified body. This event is called the Assumption of Mary. Mary, as we have seen, was a perfect human person, who was in perfect communion with God. Therefore, she experienced at the end of her earthly life what everyone who is saved will experience at the end of time when their bodies are glorified in heaven and reunited with their souls. This is called the general resurrection, or the resurrection of the dead. The Catechism puts it this way:

> "Finally the Immaculate Virgin, preserved free from all stain
> of original sin, when the course of her earthly life was finished,
> was taken up body and soul into heavenly glory, and exalted
> by the Lord as Queen over all things, so that she might be the
> more fully conformed to her Son, the Lord of lords and con-
> queror of sin and death" [LG 59; cf. Pius XII, Munificentissimus

Deus (1950): DS 3903; cf. Rev 19:16]. The Assumption of the Blessed Virgin is a singular participation in her Son's Resurrection and an anticipation of the resurrection of other Christians. (CCC 966)

The Perpetual Virginity of Mary

The Church has always taught that Mary was not just a virgin when she conceived Jesus, but that she remained a virgin throughout her life. This "perpetual virginity" is a part of our understanding of her profound sanctity. Many Protestants deny this doctrine. They argue that the Bible itself speaks of Jesus' brothers (Matt 12:46–47; 13:55; Gal 1:19). In the Bible, however, the word "brother" is often used to mean a close male relative such as a cousin. It is in this sense, the Church has always taught, that the Bible speaks of "brothers of the Lord."

There are several reasons why we believe in Mary's perpetual virginity. First, it is the received Tradition of the Church that Mary had no other children and remained a virgin her whole life. And, in fact, the New Testament does not explicitly say that those who are referred to as brothers and sisters of Jesus are sons of Mary. Furthermore, if Mary had had other sons, why would Jesus have assigned St. John the task of caring for her after his death (John 19:26)? This task would certainly have fallen to one of her other sons. Likewise, the "brothers of the Lord" are named James, Joseph, Simon, and Judas (these are not the Apostles Simon and Judas). Matthew 27:56 and Mark 15:40, however, tell us that there was another Mary who stood with Jesus' mother at the foot of the Cross and that this woman was the mother of James and Joseph. It seems likely that this other Mary was a close relative to the Virgin Mary, and so her sons would have been considered cousins or "brethren" of Christ.

There are several other ways of understanding the New Testament's mention of Christ's brothers, but what is really important is to see that the Bible certainly does not clearly teach that Mary had other children.

Mary, Mother of the Church

Mary is the mother of Jesus, and since the Church is the Body of Christ, made up of his adopted brothers and sisters, Mary is also the Mother of the Church. Recall Jesus' words on the Cross: "When Jesus saw his mother, and the disciple whom he loved standing near, he said to his mother, 'Woman, behold, your son!' Then he said to the disciple, 'Behold, your mother!' And from that hour the disciple took her to his own home" (John 19:26–27).

In addition to seeing Mary as its mother, the Church also sees Mary as its model. Mary, after all, was totally faithful; she was the first disciple of Jesus. Likewise, the Church itself is totally faithful, and each of the baptized within it are called to total faithfulness. Similarly, Mary brought forth Jesus to the world. The Church, too, brings forth Jesus to the world, both sacramentally in the Eucharist and in proclaiming his Gospel through word and example. Another parallel is that Mary was the perfect mother; she loved her Son to the end and suffered with him. The Church also loves her children to the end and is willing to suffer martyrdom for them. In all these ways, Mary is both the Mother of the Church and the model for the Church. She was the first Christian and the first disciple. With Jesus in her womb, she was a Church of one.

Today, with this understanding of Mary as the Mother of God, the Mother of the Church, and our Mother, her cooperation in the plan of redemption can serve as a model for our cooperation with God in the building up of his kingdom.

SELECTED READING:
Second Vatican Council, Dogmatic Constitution on the Church *Lumen Gentium* (November 21, 1964), nos. 53–61

The Virgin Mary, who at the message of the angel received the Word of God in her heart and in her body and gave Life to the world, is acknowledged and honored as being truly the Mother of God and Mother of the Redeemer. Redeemed by reason of the merits of her

Son and united to Him by a close and indissoluble tie, she is endowed with the high office and dignity of being the Mother of the Son of God, by which account she is also the beloved daughter of the Father and the temple of the Holy Spirit. Because of this gift of sublime grace she far surpasses all creatures, both in heaven and on earth. At the same time, however, because she belongs to the offspring of Adam she is one with all those who are to be saved. She is "the mother of the members of Christ . . . having cooperated by charity that faithful might be born in the Church, who are members of that Head." Wherefore she is hailed as a pre-eminent and singular member of the Church, and as its type and excellent exemplar in faith and charity. The Catholic Church, taught by the Holy Spirit, honors her with filial affection and piety as a most beloved mother. . . .

The Sacred Scriptures of both the Old and the New Testament, as well as ancient Tradition show the role of the Mother of the Saviour in the economy of salvation in an ever clearer light and draw attention to it. The books of the Old Testament describe the history of salvation, by which the coming of Christ into the world was slowly prepared. These earliest documents, as they are read in the Church and are understood in the light of a further and full revelation, bring the figure of the woman, Mother of the Redeemer, into a gradually clearer light. When it is looked at in this way, she is already prophetically foreshadowed in the promise of victory over the serpent which was given to our first parents after their fall into sin. Likewise she is the Virgin who shall conceive and bear a son, whose name will be called Emmanuel. She stands out among the poor and humble of the Lord, who confidently hope for and receive salvation from Him. With her the exalted Daughter of Sion, and after a long expectation of the promise, the times are fulfilled and the new Economy established, when the Son of God took a human nature from her, that He might in the mysteries of His flesh free man from sin.

The Father of mercies willed that the incarnation should be preceded by the acceptance of her who was predestined to be the mother of His Son, so that just as a woman contributed to death, so also a woman should contribute to life. That is true in outstanding fashion of the mother of Jesus, who gave to the world Him who is Life itself and who renews all things, and who was enriched by God with the gifts which befit such a role. It is no wonder therefore that the usage prevailed among the Fathers whereby they called the mother of God entirely holy and free from all stain of sin, as though fashioned by the Holy Spirit and formed as a new creature. Adorned from the first instant of her conception with the radiance of an entirely unique holiness, the Virgin of Nazareth is greeted, on God's command, by an angel messenger as "full of grace," and to the heavenly messenger she replies: "Behold the handmaid of the Lord, be it done unto me according to thy word." Thus Mary, a daughter of Adam, consenting to the divine Word, became the mother of Jesus, the one and only Mediator. Embracing God's salvific will with a full heart and impeded by no sin, she devoted herself totally as a handmaid of the Lord to the person and work of her Son, under Him and with Him, by the grace of almighty God, serving the mystery of redemption. Rightly therefore the holy Fathers see her as used by God not merely in a passive way, but as freely cooperating in the work of human salvation through faith and obedience. For, as St. Irenaeus says, she "being obedient, became the cause of salvation for herself and for the whole human race." Hence not a few of the early Fathers gladly assert in their preaching, "The knot of Eve's disobedience was untied by Mary's obedience; what the virgin Eve bound through her unbelief, the Virgin Mary loosened by her faith." Comparing Mary with Eve, they call her "the Mother of the living," and still more often they say: "death through Eve, life through Mary."

This union of the Mother with the Son in the work of salvation is made manifest from the time of Christ's virginal conception up to His death it is shown first of all when Mary, arising in haste to go to visit Elizabeth, is greeted by her as blessed because of her belief in the promise of salvation and the precursor leaped with joy in the womb of his mother. This union is manifest also at the birth of Our Lord, who did not diminish His mother's virginal integrity but sanctified it, when the Mother of God joyfully showed her firstborn Son to the shepherds and Magi. When she presented Him to the Lord in the temple, making the offering of the poor, she heard Simeon fore-telling at the same time that her Son would be a sign of contradiction and that a sword would pierce the mother's soul, that out of many hearts thoughts might be revealed. When the Child Jesus was lost and they had sought Him sorrowing, His parents found Him in the temple, taken up with the things that were His Father's business; and they did not understand the word of their Son. His Mother indeed kept these things to be pondered over in her heart.

In the public life of Jesus, Mary makes significant appearances. This is so even at the very beginning, when at the marriage feast of Cana, moved with pity, she brought about by her intercession the beginning of miracles of Jesus the Messiah. In the course of her Son's preaching she received the words whereby in extolling a kingdom beyond the calculations and bonds of flesh and blood, He declared blessed those who heard and kept the word of God, as she was faith-fully doing. After this manner the Blessed Virgin advanced in her pilgrimage of faith, and faithfully persevered in her union with her Son unto the cross, where she stood, in keeping with the divine plan, grieving exceedingly with her only begotten Son, uniting herself with a maternal heart with His sacrifice, and lovingly consenting to the immolation of this Victim which she herself had brought forth. Finally, she was given by the same Christ Jesus dying on the cross as a mother to His disciple with these words: "Woman, behold thy son."

But since it has pleased God not to manifest solemnly the mystery of the salvation of the human race before He would pour forth the Spirit promised by Christ, we see the apostles before the day of Pentecost "persevering with one mind in prayer with the women and Mary the Mother of Jesus, and with His brethren," and Mary by her prayers imploring the gift of the Spirit, who had already overshadowed her in the Annunciation. Finally, the Immaculate Virgin, preserved free from all guilt of original sin, on the comple-tion of her earthly sojourn, was taken up body and soul into heavenly glory, and exalted by the Lord as Queen of the universe, that she might be the more fully conformed to her Son, the Lord of lords and the conqueror of sin and death.

There is but one Mediator as we know from the words of the apostle, "for there is one God and one mediator of God and men, the man Christ Jesus, who gave himself [as] a redemption for all." The maternal duty of Mary toward men in no wise obscures or diminishes this unique mediation of Christ, but rather shows His power. For all the salvific influence of the Blessed Virgin on men originates, not from some inner necessity, but from the divine pleasure. It flows forth from the superabundance of the merits of Christ, rests on His mediation, depends entirely on it and draws all its power from it. In no way does it impede, but rather does it foster the immediate union of the faithful with Christ.

Predestined from eternity by that decree of divine providence which determined the incarnation of the Word to be the Mother of God, the Blessed Virgin was on this earth the virgin Mother of the Redeemer, and above all others and in a singular way the generous associate and humble handmaid of the Lord. She conceived, brought forth and nourished Christ. She presented Him to the Father in the temple, and was united with Him by compassion as He died on the Cross. In this singular way she cooperated by her obedience, faith, hope and burning charity in the work of the Saviour in giving back supernatural life to souls. Wherefore she is our mother in the order of grace.

This maternity of Mary in the order of grace began with the consent which she gave in faith at the Annunciation and which she sustained without wavering beneath the cross, and lasts until the eternal fulfillment of all the elect. Taken up to heaven she did not lay aside this salvific duty, but by her constant intercession continued to bring us the gifts of eternal salvation. By her maternal charity, she cares for the brethren of her Son, who still journey on earth surrounded by dangers and cultics, until they are led into the happiness of their true home. Therefore the Blessed Virgin is invoked by the Church under the titles of Advocate, Auxiliatrix, Adjutrix, and Mediatrix. This, however, is to be so understood that it neither takes away from nor adds anything to the dignity and efficaciousness of Christ the one Mediator.

For no creature could ever be counted as equal with the Incarnate Word and Redeemer. Just as the priesthood of Christ is shared in various ways both by the ministers and by the faithful, and as the one goodness of God is really communicated in different ways to His creatures, so also the unique mediation of the Redeemer does not exclude but rather gives rise to a manifold cooperation which is but a sharing in this one source.

The Church does not hesitate to profess this subordinate role of Mary. It knows it through unfailing experience of it and commends it to the hearts of the faithful, so that encouraged by this maternal help they may the more intimately adhere to the Mediator and Redeemer.

QUESTIONS FOR REVIEW

1. What does the dogma of the Immaculate Conception hold?
2. What does the dogma of Mary's Perpetual Virginity hold?
3. Name two reasons why references to Jesus' brothers in the Scriptures don't necessarily mean Mary had other children.
4. What does the dogma of the Ascension hold?
5. How is Mary a model for the Church?

QUESTIONS FOR DISCUSSION

1. Describe your relationship with Mary. Do you talk to her? Try to imitate her? Why or why not?
2. Mary is your mother in heaven. Is that an easy concept or difficult concept for you to understand and why?
3. What are two ways you could imitate Mary more readily in your everyday life?

Part III

THE MYSTERY OF THE INCARNATION

Chapter 1

JESUS: FULLY GOD
AND FULLY MAN

	ASSIGNED READING
	Matthew 1:12–25
	John 20:19–31
	Philippians 2:1–11
	1 Corinthians 15:42–50
	1 John 1
	CCC 4614–4669
	CCC 522–540

Sometimes, the most basic truth of Christianity is too much to get our minds around: God became our brother. That's an astounding thing. No other religion makes this claim. In Greek and Roman mythology, the gods came down to earth to meddle and to frustrate humanity—not to become human. In other major religions, such as Islam, God is so far above and beyond the world that the idea of God becoming man is inconceivable. Only in Christianity does God, as part of the economy of salvation, take on our human nature and become man.

As we saw in Part II, this was such a challenging idea that it took several hundred years for the Church to learn how to articulate it properly. The Incarnation is a great mystery. It also is the very center of the Christian understanding of all reality. In the Incarnation, God and man, heaven and earth, come together. It is the event that gives all other events meaning. For this reason, it was extremely important that the Church get its articulation of that mystery right and be able to precisely say that the eternal God became totally and completely a man without sacrificing any of his divinity; that the man Jesus remained totally God.

When we understand that, it makes his invitation to us all the more remarkable: the man who was God invites us to be his part of his family, that is to say, to become the sons and daughters of God the Father. This is salvation.

> "What he was, he remained and what he was not, he assumed" [LH, 1 January, Antiphon for Morning Prayer; cf. St. Leo the Great, *Sermo in nat. Dom.* 1, 2; PL 54, 191–192], sings the Roman Liturgy. And the liturgy of St. John Chrysostom proclaims and sings: "O only-begotten Son and Word of God, immortal being, you who deigned for our salvation to become incarnate of the holy Mother of God and ever-virgin Mary, you who without change became man and were crucified, O Christ our God, you who by your death have crushed death, you who are one of the Holy Trinity, glorified with the Father and the Holy Spirit, save us!" [Liturgy of St. John Chrysostom, Troparion "*O monogenes.*"]. (CCC 469)

While Jesus remained who he was from all eternity, the divine Son of God, in time and history he was "incarnate of the virgin Mary" (Nicene Creed). This means he took on our human nature and lived an entirely human life:

> For by His incarnation the Son of God has united Himself in some fashion with every man. He worked with human hands, He thought with a human mind, acted by human choice and

loved with a human heart. Born of the Virgin Mary, He has truly been made one of us, like us in all things except sin.[1]

When we say Jesus lived an entirely human life this is saying that Jesus is like us "in all things but sin" (Heb 4:15). He demonstrated this humanity in every aspect of his earthly life and had many common human experiences. Consider the following:

Family

Like you and me, Jesus had a family, Mary and Joseph—the Holy Family. He grew up with them, was taught by them, and traveled with them (see Luke 2:41–52). He also had an extended family: John the Baptist was a cousin and James and Joseph (Matt 13:55; 28:1; cf. 27:56), the "brothers of the Lord," were sons of a close relative whom Matthew calls "the other Mary." The fact that Jesus had close relatives with whom he grew up and spent time means that he had the same familial experiences we have. This is important because it affirms that the human family is itself good and is a part of God's plan for humanity. God created us to live as families. He wants us to live as families, and he wants this because our families are a part of what it means to be created in the image of God (Gen 1:27–28). When Jesus became a human being, he became a little baby, then a child, an adolescent, and then a man in his prime. He had a mother and a foster father. The family part of his life is integral to his human life. Without it, Christ would have missed something of what it means to be human.

---

[1] Second Vatican Council, Pastoral Constitution on the Church in the Modern World *Gaudium et Spes* (December 7, 1965), §22.

SELECTED READING:
Second Vatican Council, Pastoral Constitution on the
Church in the Modern World *Gaudium et Spes* (December
7, 1965), no. 48

The intimate partnership of married life and love has been established by the Creator and qualified by His laws, and is rooted in the
conjugal covenant of irrevocable personal consent. Hence by that
human act whereby spouses mutually bestow and accept each other
a relationship arises which by divine will and in the eyes of society
too is a lasting one. For the good of the spouses and their off-springs
as well as of society, the existence of the sacred bond no longer
depends on human decisions alone. For, God Himself is the author
of matrimony, endowed as it is with various benefits and purposes.
All of these have a very decisive bearing on the continuation of the
human race, on the personal development and eternal destiny of the
individual members of a family, and on the dignity, stability, peace
and prosperity of the family itself and of human society as a whole.
By their very nature, the institution of matrimony itself and conjugal
love are ordained for the procreation and education of children, and
find in them their ultimate crown. Thus a man and a woman, who
by their compact of conjugal love "are no longer two, but one flesh"
(Matt. 19:ff), render mutual help and service to each other through
an intimate union of their persons and of their actions. Through this
union they experience the meaning of their oneness and attain to it
with growing perfection day by day. As a mutual gift of two persons,
this intimate union and the good of the children impose total fidelity
on the spouses and argue for an unbreakable oneness between them.

Christ the Lord abundantly blessed this many-faceted love,
welling up as it does from the fountain of divine love and structured
as it is on the model of His union with His Church. For as God of
old made Himself present to His people through a covenant of love
and fidelity, so now the Savior of men and the Spouse of the Church
comes into the lives of married Christians through the sacrament of
matrimony. He abides with them thereafter so that just as He loved

the Church and handed Himself over on her behalf, the spouses may love each other with perpetual fidelity through mutual self-bestowal.

Authentic married love is caught up into divine love and is governed and enriched by Christ's redeeming power and the saving activity of the Church, so that this love may lead the spouses to God with powerful effect and may aid and strengthen them in sublime office of being a father or a mother. For this reason Christian spouses have a special sacrament by which they are fortified and receive a kind of consecration in the duties and dignity of their state. By virtue of this sacrament, as spouses fulfill their conjugal and family obligation, they are penetrated with the spirit of Christ, which suffuses their whole lives with faith, hope and charity. Thus they increasingly advance the perfection of their own personalities, as well as their mutual sanctification, and hence contribute jointly to the glory of God.

As a result, with their parents leading the way by example and family prayer, children and indeed everyone gathered around the family hearth will find a readier path to human maturity, salvation and holiness. Graced with the dignity and office of fatherhood and motherhood, parents will energetically acquit themselves of a duty which devolves primarily on them, namely education and especially religious education.

As living members of the family, children contribute in their own way to making their parents holy. For they will respond to the kindness of their parents with sentiments of gratitude, with love and trust. They will stand by them as children should when hardships overtake their parents and old age brings its loneliness. Widowhood, accepted bravely as a continuation of the marriage vocation, should be esteemed by all. Families too will share their spiritual riches generously with other families. Thus the Christian family, which springs from marriage as a reflection of the loving covenant uniting Christ with the Church, and as a participation in that covenant, will manifest to all men Christ's living presence in the world, and the genuine nature of the Church. This the family will do by the mutual love of the spouses, by their generous fruitfulness, their solidarity and faithfulness, and by the loving way in which all members of the family assist one another.

Friends

Also like us, Jesus had friends with whom he spent time: Martha, Mary, and Lazarus (see John 11:17–27; Luke 10:38–42; John 11:1–11ff.). Jesus wept when Lazarus died (John 11:35) and gave Martha advice (Luke 10:41). Then, there were the Twelve Apostles, his closest friends (see Matt 10:1–4). Jesus "hung out" with his friends. He ate with them, lived with them, and had common experiences with them. Ultimately, he died for them. To his Apostles at the Last Supper, Jesus said:

> Greater love has no man than this, that a man lay down his life for his friends. You are my friends if you do what I command you. No longer do I call you servants, for the servant does not know what his master is doing; but I have called you friends, for all that I have heard from my Father I have made known to you. (John 15:13–15)

It was a part of Christ's Incarnational mission to befriend us. St. Thomas Aquinas wrote:

> Friendship is based on a certain equality, and consequently it would seem that those who are very unequal cannot be united in friendship. And so, that friendship between man and God might be more intimate, it was well for man that God should become man—since friendship between man and man is natural—in order that by knowing a God made visible to us, we might be drawn to the love of things invisible.[2]

As was the case with the family, Jesus' friendships show us that friendship is itself good and a part of the divine plan. We should have friends. But, we need to love them for their own sake and not treat them as a means for our pleasure or enjoyment. Jesus died for his friends. He

---

[2] Thomas Aquinas, *Summa Contra Gentiles*, trans. the English Dominican Fathers (New York: Benziger Brothers, 1929), 4.54.

died for us. He did not take advantage of us, and he most certainly was not indifferent to our suffering. His whole mission was focused on bringing us to true happiness. We need to treat our own friends in the same loving, considerate way.

Work

When God became man, he had a job: he was a carpenter. His foster father Joseph was a carpenter, and Jesus followed in his foster father's footsteps (Mark 6:3; Matt 13:55). The work Jesus did as a carpenter is an example to us. It shows us that our labor is a participation in God's creation. God delighted in his creation when he made the world, which the book of Genesis referred to as God's "work" or "craftsmanship" (*melakhah*; Gen 2:2). He wants us to have fulfilling work too, work that builds up his kingdom on earth.

Oftentimes, cultural representations of work depict it as a meaningless drudgery that people have to do just to get by; but, that isn't anything like the purpose God has in mind for our labor. While it's true that we experience suffering in our work as a result of original sin (Gen 3:17), even before the Fall, God "took the man and put him in the garden of Eden to *till it and keep it*" (Gen 2:15; emphasis added). When we work, we create new things, and so our work is yet another example of us being made in the image of God. Jesus participated fully in this aspect of our humanity.

SELECTED READING:
John Paul II, Encyclical Letter on Human Work *Laborem Exercens* (September 14, 1981), no. 4

The Church is convinced that work is a fundamental dimension of man's existence on earth. She is confirmed in this conviction by considering the whole heritage of the many sciences devoted to man: anthropology, palaeontology, history, sociology, psychology and so on; they all seem to bear witness to this reality in an irrefutable way.

But the source of the Church's conviction is above all the revealed word of God, and therefore what is *a conviction of the intellect* is also *a conviction of faith*. The reason is that the Church—and it is worthwhile stating it at this point—believes in man: she thinks of man and addresses herself to him *not only* in the light of historical experience, not only with the aid of the many methods of scientific knowledge, but in the first place in the light of the revealed word of the living God. Relating herself to man, she seeks to express the eternal designs and transcendent destiny which the *living God*, the Creator and Redeemer, has linked with him.

The Church finds *in the very first pages of the Book of Genesis* the source of her conviction that work is a fundamental dimension of human existence on earth. An analysis of these texts makes us aware that they express—sometimes in an archaic way of manifesting thought—the fundamental truths about man, in the context of the mystery of creation itself. These truths are decisive for man from the very beginning, and at the same time they trace out the main lines of his earthly existence, both in the state of original justice and also after the breaking, caused by sin, of the Creator's original covenant with creation in man. When man, who had been created "in the image of God. . . . male and female," hears the words: "Be fruitful and *multiply, and fill the earth and subdue* it," even though these words do not refer directly and explicitly to work, beyond any doubt they indirectly indicate it as an activity for man to carry out in the world. Indeed, they show its very deepest essence. Man is the image of God partly through the mandate received from his Creator to subdue, to dominate, the earth. In carrying out this mandate, man, every human being, reflects the very action of the Creator of the universe.

Work understood as a "transitive" activity, that is to say an activity beginning in the human subject and directed towards an external object, presupposes a specific dominion by man over "the earth," and in its turn it confirms and develops this dominion. It is clear that the term "the earth" of which the biblical text speaks is to be understood in the first place as that fragment of the visible universe that man inhabits. By extension, however, it can be understood as the whole of the visible world insofar as it comes within the range of man's influence and of his striving to satisfy his needs. The expression "subdue the earth" has an immense range. It means all the resources that the earth (and indirectly the visible world) contains and which, through the conscious activity of man, can be discovered and used for his ends. And so these words, placed at the beginning of the Bible, never cease to be relevant. They embrace equally the past ages of civilization and economy, as also the whole of modern reality and future phases of development, which are perhaps already to some extent beginning to take shape, though for the most part they are still almost unknown to man and hidden from him.

While people sometimes speak of periods of "acceleration" in the economic life and civilization of humanity or of individual nations, linking these periods to the progress of science and technology and especially to discoveries which are decisive for social and economic life, at the same time it can be said that none of these phenomena of "acceleration" exceeds the essential content of what was said in that most ancient of biblical texts. As man, through his work, becomes more and more the master of the earth, and as he confirms his dominion over the visible world, again through his work, he nevertheless remains in every case and at every phase of this process within the Creator's original ordering. And this ordering remains necessarily and indissolubly linked with the fact that man was created, as male and female, "in the image of God." This process is, at the same time, universal: it embraces all human beings, every generation, every phase of economic and cultural development, and at the same time it is a process that takes place within each human being, in each conscious human subject. Each and every individual is at the same time embraced by it. Each and every individual, to the proper extent and in an incalculable number of ways, takes part in the giant process whereby man "subdues the earth" through his work.

Food

Both before and after his Resurrection, Jesus ate and drank. Eating and drinking were so tied to the Jewish culture that the experience of community gathered around a table was a key tool for evangelization. Jesus would often eat with people he did not agree with (see Luke 7:36ff.; 14:1ff.), and he looked forward to a good meal with friends (Luke 22:15).

Food likewise had a very important place in Jesus' ministry. Consider the number of times we hear about food, especially bread, in the Gospels. For example, when Jesus fasted in the desert, he got hungry and the devil tempted him with bread (Luke 4:2–3). Later, he told us to pray in the Our Father, "Give us this day our daily bread" (Matt 6:11; 15:36). He also multiplied the loaves to feed thousands of people (Matt 14:19); referred to the kingdom of God as a wedding banquet (Matt 22:2–3; Rev 19:9), and Jesus even referred to himself as the bread of life, as the food that will make us live forever (John 6:35).

This, of course, is in reference to the Eucharist, the sacrament in which Jesus gives himself to us under the appearance of bread (Matt 26:26; Mark 14:22; Luke 22:19; 1 Cor 11:24). The Church describes the Eucharist as the very source and summit of the Christian life (CCC 1324). At the Mass, through consuming the food that is Jesus, we are united with God and with each other. In this, we see the centrality of food to Jesus' mission. We also see that Christianity doesn't have any disdain for the body. Rather, through the Incarnation and its perpetuation in the Eucharist, God has demonstrated that our bodies are great gifts. They are good. They also are central to the economy of salvation.

Jesus enjoyed eating and drinking with his friends because sustaining our bodies is part of what it means to be human. And in the Eucharist, sustenance for the body and sustenance for the soul come from one and the same meal.

SELECTED READING:
Emily Stimpson Chapman, *The Catholic Table*, pp. 43–45

Nowhere are the bonds between food and the love of God more evident than in the Eucharist.

In the Mass, bread and wine become Body and Blood. In Holy Communion, Jesus Christ gives himself to us as real food and real drink.

The Eucharist is not a symbol of Jesus Christ; it is Jesus Christ. It is the greatest miracle any of us will ever witness and the greatest gift any of us will ever receive. We feed on God so that we can share his life and become what he is.

Food, however, when understood in the light of the Eucharist, is one, big, fat symbol.

Every natural truth about food—food as a source of community, comfort, love, healing, and joy—ultimately points beyond itself to what happens every day in every Catholic church in the world. So . . .

Food creates and sustains community. The Eucharist incorporates us into the ultimate community, the family of God, the Body of Christ.

Food comforts us, making us forget our troubles for a moment. The Eucharist consoles us on an infinitely deeper level, helping us join our sufferings to the suffering of the crucified Christ and exchange our heavy yoke for his much lighter one.

Food signifies love, allowing us to show others how much we care for them. The Eucharist is Love. It's God's complete gift of himself to us.

Food goes hand in hand with sacrifice; it always requires work. The Eucharist is the re-presentation of the greatest sacrifice the world has ever known. It cuts across space and time, allowing each of us to be mystically present on Calvary, where the God of the Universe sacrificed his life for our fallen, broken selves.

Food heals; it strengthens our bodies and our minds. The Eucharist heals too; it heals our souls. It wipes away venial sins and nourishes us with the life of Christ, enabling virtue to grow.

Lastly, food brings joy, but only fleeting, passing, momentary joy. The Eucharist—received frequently, reverently, worthily—brings us the everlasting joy of eternal life with Christ.

Again, the Eucharist isn't the symbol. The symbol is food.

From the beginning, God knew he would become man and die on a cross. He knew he would give himself to us, body to body, flesh to flesh. The Eucharist wasn't some plan he dreamed up a few thousand years into man's existence. Becoming bread wasn't a scheme he concocted on the fly, after watching the Israelites screw things up one too many times.

God is eternal. He is infinite. He is outside of time. From all eternity, he knew how this whole salvation history drama would play out. Accordingly, food's role in that drama is not a coincidence. It's not happenstance. Food's ability to be both what it is and more than it is, to shed light on natural truths about man and supernatural truths about God, is all by design. God made it that way from the beginning. God always meant for food to be an ordinary sign that would point beyond itself to the extraordinary reality of the Eucharist. God always meant food to be a natural symbol of the very greatest supernatural truths.

This is how the world works. This is reality. This is what a sacramental worldview helps us see. It reveals to us the glory, the majesty, and the mystery contained within a plain piece of bread. It helps us recognize that God wants every meal, every supper to be a foreshadowing and foretaste of the feast to end all feasts: the Marriage Supper of the Lamb.

Temptation

Jesus didn't just enjoy the good parts of human existence, such as family, friends, and food. He also embraced the difficult parts. One of those is temptation. In the desert, at the beginning of his public ministry, Jesus was tempted in the desert by the devil (Matt 4:1–12). He wasn't tempted in the sense that he considered doing something wrong, but in the sense that the devil put him to the test. The devil presented him with the option of an "easier" path than that of the will of God—a path that he immediately rejected in favor of the suffering that lay before him. That's where Jesus differed from us. When Satan tested Adam, the man failed. When Satan tested Jesus, the man was victorious. He endured temptation, but he endured it without sin (Heb 4:15). He never gave into it. Still, even without the sin that we normally associate with the entertaining of temptations, this must have been a painful experience.

Chapter 2

Sorrow, Suffering, and Death

ASSIGNED READING
Matthew 26:36–47
Matthew 8:14–17
CCC 1503–1505

Jesus also experienced the emotions of sorrow and distress, particularly the night before his Crucifixion. During the Agony in the Garden, he contemplated the tortuous death that he was about to experience and felt deeply troubled, so much so that he sweated drops of blood. While Jesus' will never deviated from the will of God, that doesn't mean that he wouldn't have liked to avoid the physical pain that awaited him. He knew what was coming, and it grieved his heart.

Even more than the physical suffering, Jesus suffered when his closest friends let him down. During his Agony in the Garden, Jesus grew frustrated when Peter, John, and James couldn't manage to stay awake with him. Then, one of his closest followers, one of the Twelve Apostles, Judas, betrayed him outright, arriving at the garden at the head of a mob. When Jesus referred to Judas as "friend" and asked him what he was doing (Matt 26:47–51), can we not hear the sadness in his voice? That same night, as Jesus was being mocked and beaten, St. Peter denied even knowing him, not once but three times. At the third denial, "the Lord turned and looked at Peter" (Luke 22:61). This must have been a moment of extreme sorrow for the Lord, one to which, unfortunately, so many of us can relate.

Death and sickness are a constant of human life, and Jesus didn't avoid them either. In fact, he spent much of his ministry healing the sick and helping outcasts (see Matt 8:13, Luke 14:4ff., John 4:47ff., Luke 5:12ff.). In doing so, he personified compassion. The word "compassion" literally means "to suffer with," and this is just what Jesus did. When he saw those who were hurting, he hurt with them. This is the nature of love. When you love someone, their joy is your joy, and their pain is your pain. God loves us completely. He feels our pain in a more direct and real way than even we do. Jesus, in the Incarnation, shows us this is true. He healed people, he helped them, and ultimately he went to the Cross and died for them. That death was both excruciatingly painful and humiliating. Because of it, not one of us, when we're hurting, can say, "God doesn't know what I'm going through!" He does. He has been there. And he remains ever ready to help us, heal us, and carry us as we carry our cross.

SELECTED READING:
John Paul II, Apostolic Letter on the Christian Meaning of Human Suffering *Salvifici Doloris* (February 11, 1984), no. 16

In his messianic activity in the midst of Israel, Christ drew increasingly closer to the world of human suffering. "He went about doing good," and his actions concerned primarily those who were suffering and seeking help. He healed the sick, consoled the afflicted, fed the hungry, freed people from deafness, from blindness, from leprosy, from the devil and from various physical disabilities, three times he restored the dead to life. He was sensitive to every human suffering, whether of the body or of the soul. And at the same time he taught, and at the heart of his teaching there are the eight beatitudes, which are addressed to people tried by various sufferings in their temporal life. These are "the poor in spirit" and "the afflicted" and "those who hunger and thirst for justice" and those who are "persecuted for justice sake," when they insult them, persecute them and speak falsely every kind of evil against them for the sake of Christ . . . Thus according to Matthew; Luke mentions explicitly those "who hunger now."

At any rate, Christ drew close above all to the world of human suffering through the fact of having taken this suffering upon his very self. During his public activity, he experienced not only fatigue, homelessness, misunderstanding even on the part of those closest to him, but, more than anything, he became progressively more and more isolated and encircled by hostility and the preparations for putting him to death. Christ is aware of this, and often speaks to his disciples of the sufferings and death that await him: "Behold, we are going up to Jerusalem; and the Son of man will be delivered to the chief priests and the scribes, and they will condemn him to death and deliver him to the Gentiles; and they will mock him, and spit upon him, and scourge him, and kill him; and after three days he will rise." Christ goes towards his Passion and death with full awareness of the mission that he has to fulfil precisely in this way. Precisely by means of this suffering he must bring it about "that man should not perish, but have eternal life." Precisely by means of his Cross, he must strike at the roots of evil, planted in the history of man and in human souls. Precisely by means of his Cross, he must accomplish the work of salvation. This work, in the plan of eternal Love, has a redemptive character.

And therefore Christ severely reproves Peter when the latter wants to make him abandon the thoughts of suffering and of death on the Cross. And when, during his arrest in Gethsemane, the same Peter tries to defend him with the sword, Christ says, "Put your sword back into its place . . . But how then should the scriptures be fulfilled, that it must be so?" And he also says, "Shall I not drink the cup which the Father has given me?" This response, like others that reappear in different points of the Gospel, shows how profoundly Christ was imbued by the thought that he had already expressed in the conversation with Nicodemus: "For God so loved the world that he gave his only Son, that whoever believes in him should not perish but have eternal life." Christ goes toward his own suffering, aware of its saving power; he goes forward in obedience to the Father, but primarily he is united to the Father in this love with which he has loved the world and man in the world. And for this reason Saint Paul will write of Christ: "He loved me and gave himself for me."

In all these different ways, the Gospels portray a thoroughly human Jesus. At the same time, they portray a Jesus whose divine power is evident to the people to whom he ministered: "Where did this man get this Wisdom and these mighty works?" they ask (Matt 13:54). This union of the divine and human natures in the one Person of Jesus Christ is called the hypostatic union. The hypostatic union is not just a term from theology; it reveals God's ultimate plan for his creation. God and man are united together in the Person of Jesus Christ, and in him is revealed God's ultimate goal—to unite humanity and divinity in eternity.

The covenants, the prophets, the kings, everything that God had done for Israel, was done with the express purpose of preparing humanity for the Incarnation and Jesus' saving work. God and man are brought together in the Person of Jesus Christ, and through Jesus it becomes possible for us to become citizens of heaven, and even more, adopted sons and daughters of God. Our heavenly adoption through Baptism points forward to God's ultimate goal for creation, which is nothing short of a "new heaven" and a "new earth" (Rev 21:1–2).

Ultimately, the Incarnation affirms the immanence of God, the goodness of the human person, and the goodness of the new creation that awaits us. We have a God who knows what we go through in the course of our lives. He lived a thoroughly human life. He took no shortcuts. And he did not use his divinity as a crutch to get through the many difficulties of being a man. Rather, Jesus used his divinity to show how a thoroughly human life, when lived for God, takes on a divine quality (2 Pet 1:4). In effect, he shows us how life is meant to be lived by all of us.

QUESTIONS FOR REVIEW

1.   What does Jesus tell us is the greatest love a person can have for their friends?
2.   How did original sin change our experience of work?
3.   Why did food play such a prominent role in Jesus' ministry?
4.   What do we mean when we say that Jesus experienced temptation?
5.   How does Jesus teach us, by his example, to respond to human suffering?

QUESTIONS FOR DISCUSSION

1.   Jesus, who was God, spent the vast majority of his life doing very ordinary things. What does this teach you about the importance of the ordinary?
2.   When you are suffering or sad, how can thinking about Jesus' own suffering help you?
3.   What about Jesus' life feels the most like your own? Why?

Part IV

JESUS CHRIST TEACHES US ABOUT OURSELVES

Chapter 1

JESUS EMBODIES WHAT HAS BEEN REVEALED IN AND THROUGH CREATION

ASSIGNED READING
John 3:16–21
Hebrews 2
Romans 5:12–21
Romans 8:1–8
Colossians 1:15–23
CCC 470–478

Jesus Christ is God made incarnate. Two thousand years ago, in the land of Israel, God himself took on a body and became a man who lived in the created world. As the Word of God, Jesus was God's perfect and complete revelation of himself. Jesus' Incarnation, therefore, embodies perfectly all that has been revealed to us in creation. It also perfectly reveals to us what it means to be human.

Jesus Shows What It Means to Be Fully Human

Each of us is made in the image and likeness of God (Gen 1:27). Through his Incarnation, Jesus confirms this. God had no problem assuming a human nature because, from the beginning, the nature of man was imprinted with the image of God. From the beginning, human nature was made to be in communion with the divine nature, and the human will was made to be in communion with the divine will. This communion became perfect in the Incarnation. The Incarnation, therefore, shows us the perfect man, who is perfectly united with God. It likewise reveals the profound dignity that is inherent in every human person (CCC 356).

> "Christ, . . . in the very revelation of the mystery of the Father and of his love, makes man fully manifest to himself and brings to light his exalted vocation" [*GS* 22]. It is in Christ, "the image of the invisible God" [*Col* 1:15; cf. *2 Cor* 4:4], that man has been created "in the image and likeness" of the Creator. It is in Christ, Redeemer and Savior, that the divine image, disfigured in man by the first sin, has been restored to its original beauty and ennobled by the grace of God [Cf. *GS* 22]. (CCC 1701)

Jesus shows us what it means to be fully human, but it's up to us to follow his example. If we're going to become the person God wants us to be and act in accord with the dignity we've been given, we must accept and maximize the gifts entrusted to us by God, particularly those gifts that reflect God himself, such as immortality, rationality and freedom, and the ability to love.

Immortality

Jesus spent his earthly ministry proclaiming the kingdom of God and pointing people to their ultimate home, heaven. "I am the resurrection and the life;" he said, "he who believes in me, though he die, yet shall he live, and whoever lives and believes in me shall never die" (John 11:25–26). It's not just Jesus' words, however, that remind us of our eternal destiny; it's also his witness. By his Resurrection, he is a constant reminder that we will rise and take up our place in the New Creation. Human beings were not created to die and disappear. We were created for eternal life. When we live in accord with God's law and seek his will, we are pursuing that life for which we were made.

Rationality and Freedom

God created man with a rational soul. This means that we are capable of knowing and understanding our world and controlling our own actions. We can distinguish truth from falsehood and right from wrong. We can look at the world around us, see our place in it, and decide what actions to take based upon what we see. In short, we have reason and free will, two things no other creature in creation can claim. Animals, unlike humans, don't have the ability to take a step back from themselves and reflect upon their motives and actions. This is why animals aren't responsible for their actions. Human beings, on the other hand, are responsible because we are capable of rational judgment. This ability to know and to choose is another way in which we are made in the image of God. God is omniscient—he knows everything. He also is omnipotent—he rules freely over everything, and there is nothing he cannot do (CCC 268). Human rationality and freedom are a small reflection of these attributes of our Creator. When we use them well, we image him more perfectly.

Jesus, as a man, also had free will and a rational soul, and he shows us what true freedom looks like. There was no conflict between the human will and the divine will in Christ. This wasn't because the divine will swallowed up the human will or forced it into subservience. Rather, in freedom, Jesus always chose the true and the good, which is precisely what the divine will desires. Both his human will and divine will were always in total agreement! God calls all of us to do the same. This isn't easy. Original sin has affected our will, so that what God wants isn't always what we want. Fortunately, the more consistently we choose God, the more our will aligns with his, and the closer our relationship becomes with him, the more free we really are.

Love

Each of us is made to love because we are made in God's image and God is love. The Persons of the Trinity love each other perfectly, and we are called to join them in that communion of love, both now and in eternity. This participation requires giving our love freely to others and to God: to love someone is by definition to give of oneself to him or her, and gifts must be freely given or they're not gifts at all. Likewise, loving as God loves means loving those who don't love us. In the Gospels, Jesus challenges us to radical discipleship by "loving our enemies" (Matt 5:44) and loving as he loved: "A new commandment I give to you, that you love one another; even as I have loved you, that you also love one another. By this all men will know that you are my disciples, if you have love for one another" (John 13:34–35).

Jesus Affirms the Goodness of Creation

Through the Incarnation, Jesus shows us our natural human gifts and talents in their perfection and reminds us to always orient them toward God. In doing so, he affirms the material aspects of human life. He affirms that our bodies are good, our minds are good, and our social lives are good.

This affirmation of our gifts and talents in the light of the Incarnation and the ministry of Christ points us toward the Church. It helps us understand why God uses the Church as the means through which we work out our salvation. In the Incarnation, God approached us in our totality, body and soul, and, in the sacraments, God continues to touch our bodies and souls. In the sacraments, he gives us grace through material means: water, oil, the laying on of hands, and the transformation of bread and wine into his Body and Blood. Grace touches our souls by touching our bodies.

It makes sense, in light of the Incarnation, that God would choose the sacraments, which always have a physical and social dimension to them, as the primary means through which he dispenses grace. It also makes sense that Jesus would have us work out our salvation together as a community united in love. The priesthood clearly and explicitly continues Jesus' earthly mission. Priests preach the good news, instruct the faithful, and forgive sins, just as Jesus did. Above all, in the Mass, they stand in for Jesus himself and make his true Incarnate Body as present today as it was in Palestine two thousand years ago. God did not just come down from heaven, spend thirty-some years here, give us some instructions, and then go away. Rather, God's presence continues in the physical world, in the midst of our human reality, through his Church, which is the mystical kingdom, whose final glory we await in anticipation.

Part of the building up of the kingdom of God "on earth as it is in heaven" (Matt 6:10) is stewardship. As we have seen, the Incarnation confirms that the created order is good. God instructed mankind to subdue the earth and to have dominion over it (Gen 1:28). God clearly placed humanity at the head of the created order. But this does not give us the right to treat his creation however we like, to abuse it or exploit it. Quite the opposite! God made us responsible for his creation. We are to live within it and be its master, and this means that we are to care for it and use its riches wisely. It is part of God's plan that we be good stewards of the earth. St. Leo the Great (400–461) wrote:

> For not only are spiritual riches and heavenly gifts received from God, but earthly and material possessions also proceed from His bounty, that He may be justified in requiring an account of those things which He has not so much put in our possession as committed to our stewardship. God's gifts, therefore, we must use properly and wisely, lest the material for good work should become an occasion of sin. For wealth, after its kind and regarded as a means, is good and is of the greatest advantage to human society, when it is in the hands of the benevolent and open-handed, and when the luxurious man does not squander

nor the miser hoard it; for whether ill-stored or unwisely spent it is equally lost.[1]

SELECTED READING:
Pope Benedict XVI, Encyclical Letter on Christian Love
Deus Caritas Est (December 25, 2005), nos. 16–18

Having reflected on the nature of love and its meaning in biblical faith, we are left with two questions concerning our own attitude: can we love God without seeing him? And can love be commanded? Against the double commandment of love these questions raise a double objection. No one has ever seen God, so how could we love him? Moreover, love cannot be commanded; it is ultimately a feeling that is either there or not, nor can it be produced by the will. Scripture seems to reinforce the first objection when it states: "If anyone says, 'I love God,' and hates his brother, he is a liar; for he who does not love his brother whom he has seen, cannot love God whom he has not seen" (*1 Jn* 4:20). But this text hardly excludes the love of God as something impossible. On the contrary, the whole context of the passage quoted from the *First Letter of John* shows that such love is explicitly demanded. The unbreakable bond between love of God and love of neighbour is emphasized. One is so closely connected to the other that to say that we love God becomes a lie if we are closed to our neighbour or hate him altogether. Saint John's words should rather be interpreted to mean that love of neighbour is a path that leads to the encounter with God, and that closing our eyes to our neighbour also blinds us to God.

True, no one has ever seen God as he is. And yet God is not totally invisible to us; he does not remain completely inaccessible. God loved us first, says the *Letter of John* quoted above (cf. 4:10), and

---

[1] Leo the Great, Sermon 10.1, in Philip Schaff and Henry Wace, eds., *Leo the Great, Gregory the Great*, A Select Library of the Nicene and Post-Nicene Fathers of the Christian Church, Second Series, vol. 12 (New York: Christian Literature Company, 1895).

this love of God has appeared in our midst. He has become visible in as much as he "has sent his only Son into the world, so that we might live through him" (*1 Jn* 4:9). God has made himself visible: in Jesus we are able to see the Father (cf. *Jn* 14:9). Indeed, God is visible in a number of ways. In the love-story recounted by the Bible, he comes towards us, he seeks to win our hearts, all the way to the Last Supper, to the piercing of his heart on the Cross, to his appearances after the Resurrection and to the great deeds by which, through the activity of the Apostles, he guided the nascent Church along its path. Nor has the Lord been absent from subsequent Church history: he encounters us ever anew, in the men and women who reflect his presence, in his word, in the sacraments, and especially in the Eucharist. In the Church's Liturgy, in her prayer, in the living community of believers, we experience the love of God, we perceive his presence and we thus learn to recognize that presence in our daily lives. He has loved us first and he continues to do so; we too, then, can respond with love. God does not demand of us a feeling which we ourselves are incapable of producing. He loves us, he makes us see and experience his love, and since he has "loved us first," love can also blossom as a response within us.

In the gradual unfolding of this encounter, it is clearly revealed that love is not merely a sentiment. Sentiments come and go. A sentiment can be a marvelous first spark, but it is not the fullness of love. Earlier we spoke of the process of purification and maturation by which *eros* comes fully into its own, becomes love in the full meaning of the word. It is characteristic of mature love that it calls into play all man's potentialities; it engages the whole man, so to speak. Contact with the visible manifestations of God's love can awaken within us a feeling of joy born of the experience of being loved. But this encounter also engages our will and our intellect. Acknowledgment of the living God is one path towards love, and the "yes" of our will to his will unites our intellect, will and sentiments in the all-embracing act of love. But this process is always open-ended; love is never "finished" and complete; throughout life, it changes and matures, and thus remains faithful to itself. *Idem velle atque idem nolle*—to want the same thing, and to reject the same thing—was recognized by antiquity as the authentic content of love: the one becomes similar to the other, and this leads to a community of will and thought. The love-story between God and man consists in the very fact that this communion of will increases in a communion of thought and sentiment, and thus our will and God's will increasingly coincide: God's will is no longer for me an alien will, something imposed on me from without by the commandments, but it is now my own will, based on the realization that God is in fact more deeply present to me than I am to myself. Then self-abandonment to God increases and God becomes our joy (cf. Ps 73 [72]:23–28).

Love of neighbour is thus shown to be possible in the way proclaimed by the Bible, by Jesus. It consists in the very fact that, in God and with God, I love even the person whom I do not like or even know. This can only take place on the basis of an intimate encounter with God, an encounter which has become a communion of will, even affecting my feelings. Then I learn to look on this other person not simply with my eyes and my feelings, but from the perspective of Jesus Christ. His friend is my friend. Going beyond exterior appearances, I perceive in others an interior desire for a sign of love, of concern. This I can offer them not only through the organizations intended for such purposes, accepting it perhaps as a political necessity. Seeing with the eyes of Christ, I can give to others much more than their outward necessities; I can give them the look of love which they crave. Here we see the necessary interplay between love of God and love of neighbour which the *First Letter of John* speaks of with such insistence. If I have no contact whatsoever with God in my life, then I cannot see in the other anything more than the other, and I am incapable of seeing in him the image of God. But if in my life I fail completely to heed others, solely out of a desire to be "devout" and to perform my "religious duties," then my relationship with God will also grow arid. It becomes merely "proper," but love less. Only my readiness to encounter my neighbour and to show him love makes me sensitive to God as well. Only if I serve my neighbour can my eyes be opened to what God does for me and how much he loves me. The saints—consider the example of Blessed Teresa of Calcutta—constantly renewed their capacity for love of neighbour from their encounter with the Eucharistic Lord, and conversely this encounter acquired its real-ism and depth in their service to others. Love of God and love of neighbour are thus inseparable, they form a single commandment. But both live from the love of God who has loved us first. No longer is it a question, then, of a "commandment" imposed from without and calling for the impossible, but rather of a freely-bestowed experience of love from within, a love which by its very nature must then be shared with others. Love grows through love. Love is "divine" because it comes from God and unites us to God; through this unifying process it makes us a "we" which transcends our divisions and makes us one, until in the end God is "all in all" (*1 Cor* 15:28).

QUESTIONS FOR REVIEW

1. What does it mean to have a rational soul?
2. What is the relationship between freedom and love?
3. How does Jesus say we must treat our enemies?
4. What is man's role in relationship to creation?
5. How do priests continue Jesus' mission through their ministry?

QUESTIONS FOR DISCUSSION

1. What does it mean to love our enemies? Have you ever seen someone do that? If so, describe.
2. God allows us to choose whether we will love him or not. What do you think this says about God?
3. The Church teaches that our bodies are good because they are created by God, loved by God, and made in his image. How is this teaching different from what the culture tells us about our bodies? Which teaching is more positive and helpful? Why?

Chapter 2

Jesus Christ Reveals the Father to Us, Who We Are, and Our Call to Holiness

ASSIGNED READING
John 15
1 John 4:7–21
CCC 512–521

Jesus Redeems Us and Gives Us His Grace

As the Catechism reminds us, "He who believes in Jesus becomes a son of God. This filial adoption transforms the believer by giving him the ability to follow the example of Christ. It makes him capable of acting rightly and being good." It then continues, "In union with his Savior, the disciple attains the perfection of charity which is holiness. Having matured in grace, the moral life blossoms into eternal life in the glory of heaven" (CCC 1709).

As we discussed at the beginning of this course, Jesus invites us to a relationship with him. When we have faith in Jesus, we respond to this invitation. Faith by necessity leads to discipleship. It can't do anything but that. Our relationship with him affects every aspect of our lives, calling us to restructure our habits, attitudes, and words in conformity with his teaching. This restructuring has its challenges, but as we struggle to conform our will to the divine will, the gap between ourselves and Christ gradually closes. This path of discipleship is the path to eternal life because Jesus is "the way, the truth, and the life" (John 14:6).

God is truly worthy of this struggle. He is worthy of all our adoration and our faith. Loving him completely is the most right thing in the world. It fulfills our human nature. When we follow Jesus in faith, we are not doing something outside of what's "normal." In fact, we are returning to what was always supposed to be normal. Without Jesus, we live in a fallen world that is dark and confusing—it was not where we were meant to live. It's not normal. What's normal is following Jesus. We were made to be in communion with God, and when we follow him, the dark world becomes, for us, light. Our path through life becomes illuminated by him. As Jesus said of himself: "I am the light of the world; he who follows me will not walk in darkness, but will have the light of life" (John 8:12).

But Jesus doesn't just call us to himself and then leave us to our own powers to figure out how to live rightly. In fact, we don't even have this power. On our own, we can't do it. We need God. We need grace. Only God can give us the grace to have faith and live rightly. Only he can give us the power to do what is right and reject what is wrong. And only he can give us the forgiveness for our sins that we need to move forward. Becoming a disciple is hard work, and we *will* fail, repeatedly. But when we do, God will always forgive us, and he will always offer us the grace to get back on track toward true discipleship. This process is called conversion.

Throughout the process of conversion we are journeying toward union with God, and it is in this union that we will find our beatitude, which means happiness. God wants this happiness for us even more than we do, and he shows us in Jesus how to attain it. He teaches us in his Word what we are to do and believe, and he provides us with all the grace, help, and forgiveness that we need in order to live up to the great call to holiness. This is the greatest of gifts.

Jesus Unites Us to God

We are all prodigal sons and daughters who have been called back to the forgiveness and love of our Father through the grace of Jesus Christ. Jesus' Incarnation reunites the whole human race to God because in him human nature is united to the divine nature. The unity of the divine and the human in Jesus also unites all of humanity with the divine.

St. Paul tells us that just as death entered the world through the sin of one man, so life is restored by one man: Adam brought death; Christ brings life (1 Cor 15:21–22). When the Son of God became a man, he united himself to the human race, while not at all severing his perfect unity with the divine Trinity. The Incarnation, therefore, forms a bridge between the human and the divine. When Christ died on the Cross, it was, in a sense, as if all humanity died on the Cross, and when he rose from the dead, it was all of humanity who defeated death.

For each of us, our victory over death begins with our Baptism, which makes us adopted sons and daughters of God. This is what we mean when we say that the people of the Church are Christ's Body. We are incorporated (incorporated means literally "put into the body") into Christ, and in doing so, we receive his Sonship as our own. Moreover, because of Christ's death and resurrection, nothing stands in our way to a real, loving, and permanent relationship with God. St. Paul writes:

> Do you not know that all of us who have been baptized into Christ Jesus were baptized into his death? We were buried therefore with him by baptism into death, so that as Christ was raised from the dead by the glory of the Father, we too might walk in newness of life. (Rom 6:3–5)

Jesus Reveals Our Call to Holiness

Through our Baptism we are conformed to Jesus. As St. Paul states, "For as many of you as were baptized into Christ have put on Christ" (Gal 3:27). This means that, in a sense, we are spiritually like him. We have become a new creation and bear his life within us. Because we are like Christ spiritually, we are called to walk in his ways, becoming more and more like him in our words and actions. Our baptism helps make this possible. It empowers us to grow in holiness and goodness.

In the Gospels, Jesus teaches us what that life of goodness consists of. Let's examine what he has to say a little more closely, starting with his teachings from the Sermon on the Mount.

The Beatitudes and the Sermon on the Mount: Matthew 5–7

Jesus, like Moses in the Old Testament, gives his followers a moral law. The heart of this moral law is found in the Sermon on the Mount (Matt 5–7). During this sermon, Jesus states that he did not come to abolish the law of Moses, but to fulfill it (Matt 5:17), and he lays out new commandments for his followers regarding anger (Matt 5:21–26), lust (Matt 5:27–30), divorce (Matt 5:31–32) and more.

Anger, Jesus, tells us, is a form of murder, lust is a form of adultery, and divorce violates God's plan for marriage. If we want to grow in holiness, he says, we must reject all three. In issuing these commands, Jesus was asking more of his listeners than the Law of Moses ever asked. He called not just for outward conformity to the law, but also inward conformity. In that, he helped us see that these commandments of his fulfill and reveal the true meaning of the commandments of the law of Moses, which is God's desire for us to conform our hearts, minds, and wills to God.

Importantly, the law that Jesus gives is not just a set of rules, but a recipe for Christian joy or beatitude. The key to Christian joy is found at the beginning of the Sermon on the Mount, in the famous sayings of Jesus known as the "Beatitudes":

1. Blessed are the poor in spirit, for theirs is the kingdom of heaven.
2. Blessed are those who mourn, for they shall be comforted.
3. Blessed are the meek, for they shall inherit the earth.

4. Blessed are those who hunger and thirst for righteousness, for they shall be satisfied.
5. Blessed are the merciful, for they shall obtain mercy.
6. Blessed are the pure in heart, for they shall see God.
7. Blessed are the peacemakers, for they shall be called sons of God.
8. Blessed are those who are persecuted for righteousness' sake, for theirs is the kingdom of heaven.

(Matt 5:2–11)

Beatitude or blessedness (in Greek, *makarios*) is sometimes translated as happiness. To be blessed is to be happy. In the Beatitudes, Jesus describes for us what it truly means to be happy. Right away, we can see that the key to happiness is not found where we usually look for it. While most people in our world expect to find happiness in money, power, prestige, and pleasure, Jesus tells us that the poor, the mourners, the meek, and those who hunger and thirst for righteousness are the ones truly blessed.

The Beatitudes give us a picture of what a life conformed to Jesus looks like. They reveal the spirit that lies behind the commandments found in the rest of the Sermon on the Mount, and they show us that the commandments are really the key to happiness. We were made to be like God and to have a relationship with God, and we only find true happiness when we keep the commandments and draw close to God in faith and prayer. Living the life described in the Beatitudes is to live a Christ-like life, and only in living that life can we find happiness and become the men and women God created us to be.

The Parables

Jesus also teaches about the life of holiness through his many parables. The parables give us practical wisdom to guide our lives and always point us toward the kingdom of God, showing us the importance of serving God and others through our actions. The Catechism says:

Jesus' invitation to enter his kingdom comes in the form of *parables*, a characteristic feature of his teaching [Cf. Mk 4:33–34]. Through his parables he invites people to the feast of the kingdom, but he also asks for a radical choice: to gain the kingdom, one must give everything [Cf. Mt 13:44–45; 22:1–14]. Words are not enough; deeds are required [Cf. Mt 21:28–32]. The parables are like mirrors for man: will he be hard soil or good earth for the word [Cf. Mt 13:3–9]? What use has he made of the talents he has received [Cf. Mt 25:14–30]? Jesus and the presence of the kingdom in this world are secretly at the heart of the parables. One must enter the kingdom, that is, become a disciple of Christ, in order to "know the secrets of the kingdom of heaven" [Mt 13:11]. For those who stay "outside," everything remains enigmatic [Mk 4:11; cf. Mt 13:10–15]. (CCC 546)

The Rich Young Man

The parables are full of deep moral teaching, but they are sometimes obscure. Even the Apostles didn't always understand what Jesus meant by them (Mark 4:10). Jesus, however, didn't always speak in parables; at times, he gave straight answers to straight questions. Once a man asked Jesus, "Good Teacher, what must I do to inherit eternal life?" (Mark 10:17). Jesus responded simply by telling him to keep the commandments (Mark 10:19). The man asserted that he had done so, and then Jesus laid out a challenge:

> And Jesus looking upon him loved him, and said to him, "You lack one thing; go, sell what you have, and give to the poor, and you will have treasure in heaven; and come, follow me." (Mark 10:21–22)

Here, Jesus helps us see that it isn't enough to keep the minimum requirements of the law and just follow the rules. Even more, Jesus calls us to be detached from the things of the world and not to allow them to get in the way of our relationship with him. Discipleship is a total commitment, and we can't hold anything back for ourselves.

This doesn't mean that all Christians are forbidden to own anything (although some people are called to this total poverty). Rather, it means we must always put our possessions in the service of our discipleship. They are a means toward the end of salvation. If we can use our riches to deepen our relationship with Jesus, even if that just happens through supporting our families and fulfilling our responsibilities to our community and the poor, this is a good thing. But, if our riches ever become something that we love for their own sake, then they have taken over what we owe to God alone.

Jesus asked the rich young man to sell his possessions and follow him, and the man couldn't. In that, he demonstrated that he loved his things more than he loved God. This is the great temptation of wealth, and Jesus directly states that it is incredibly difficult for the rich to overcome it. Thankfully, God gives us the grace we need to overcome every obstacle. With him, nothing is impossible (Mark 10:23–27).

The Two Greatest Commandments

In the Old Testament, God gave the Jews an extensive legal code to follow. They had hundreds of rules about what they could eat and when they could work and how they were called to treat family, friends, and strangers. Through the keeping of those rules they sought to become righteous. The Jews saw their legal code as the way to find favor in God's eyes. The problem was that in their desire to follow the rules, they sometimes missed the heart of those rules—they didn't understand what all those rules were about.

In the Gospels, Jesus corrects this problem by issuing the Two Greatest Commandments:

The first is, "Hear, O Israel: The Lord our God, the Lord is one;
and you shall love the Lord your God with all your heart, and
with all your soul, and with all your mind, and with all your

strength." The second is this, "You shall love your neighbor as yourself." There is no other commandment greater than these. (Mark 12:29–31)

In those two sentences, Jesus summarizes the meaning of holiness. He reminds us that the law exists to help us know how to love God and our neighbors. That love is the purpose of our life. For that love God made us, and only through fulfilling the heart of the commandments—summarized in the two greatest commandments—can we find happiness and achieve salvation. Many people in our day search for the meaning of life, but Jesus spells it out in simple terms: "Love God" and "Love your neighbor."

Our Works Will Be Judged

Many people are fascinated by what the end of the world will be like. It seems our society never gets tired of "apocalypse" movies and endless speculation about what might happen at the end of the world and when the end will come. This fascination with the end times, however, isn't new. Even during Jesus' time people wondered about it and were anxious about God's coming judgment. In fact, Jesus tells us directly what will happen in the end. Let's read Matthew 25:31–46 together.

When the Son of man comes in his glory, and all the angels with him, then he will sit on his glorious throne. Before him will be gathered all the nations, and he will separate them one from another as a shepherd separates the sheep from the goats, and he will place the sheep at his right hand, but the goats at the left. Then the King will say to those at his right hand, "Come, O blessed of my Father, inherit the kingdom prepared for you from the foundation of the world; for I was hungry and you gave me food, I was thirsty and you gave me drink, I was a stranger and you welcomed me, I was naked and you clothed me, I was sick and you visited me, I was in prison and you came to me." Then the righteous will answer him, "Lord, when did we see you hungry and feed you, or thirsty and give you drink? And when did we see you a stranger and welcome you, or naked and clothe you? And when did we see you sick or in prison and visit you?" And the King will answer them, "Truly, I say to you, as you did it to one of the least of these my brethren, you did it to me." Then he will say to those at his left hand, "Depart from me, you cursed, into the eternal fire prepared for the devil and his angels; for I was hungry and you gave me no food, I was thirsty and you gave me no drink, I was a stranger and you did not welcome me, naked and you did not clothe me, sick and in prison and you did not visit me." Then they also will answer, "Lord, when did we see you hungry or thirsty or a stranger or naked or sick or in prison, and did not minister to you?" Then he will answer them, "Truly, I say to you, as you did it not to one of the least of these, you did it not to me." And they will go away into eternal punishment, but the righteous into eternal life.

Perhaps the most important thing we hear in this passage is that we will be judged according to our works. We can't control when the world will end, but we can control what we do in the meantime. This is something that we must always remember. God is a God of great mercy and great compassion, but he also knows us to our very core. He is not tricked by our rationalizations or the arguments we make to justify our lack of concern for his commandments or for our lack of care for other people. Christian charity is not an option; it is necessary to the Christian life. The Catechism explains:

> We cannot be united with God unless we freely choose to love him. But we cannot love God if we sin gravely against him, against our neighbor or against ourselves: "He who does not love remains in death. Anyone who hates his brother is a murderer, and you know that no murderer has eternal life abiding in him" [1 Jn 3:14–15]. Our Lord warns us that we shall be separated from him if we fail to meet the serious needs of the poor and the little ones who are his brethren [Cf. Mt 25:31–46]. To die in

mortal sin without repenting and accepting God's merciful love means remaining separated from him forever by our own free choice. This state of definitive self-exclusion from communion with God and the blessed is called "hell." (CCC 1033)

The works of mercy are charitable actions by which we come to the aid of our neighbor in his spiritual and bodily necessities [Cf. *Isa* 58:6–7; *Heb* 13:3]. Instructing, advising, consoling, comforting are spiritual works of mercy, as are forgiving and bearing wrongs patiently. The corporal works of mercy consist especially in feeding the hungry, sheltering the homeless, clothing the naked, visiting the sick and imprisoned, and burying the dead [Cf. *Mt* 25:31–46]. Among all these, giving alms to the poor is one of the chief witnesses to fraternal charity: it is also a work of justice pleasing to God [Cf. *Tob* 4:5–11; *Sir* 17:22; *Mt* 6:2–4]. (CCC 2447)

Through his teachings, Jesus Christ tells us how to become ever more conformed to him. He gives us a guidebook to holiness. Discipleship requires that we listen to his teaching and do as he tells us. We trust that God as our creator knows what is good for us better than we can know for ourselves. He knows us perfectly, and when he became Incarnate as Jesus Christ, he actually became one of us. His teaching is not obscure or hard to understand. It is simple and straightforward, but it can be very difficult to practice it. In order to live up to the demands of discipleship, we must rely on God's grace, turning to him for help through prayer.

Jesus Teaches Us to Pray

When we pray, we seek communion with God through conversation with him. Prayer is that conversation. It is the raising of our minds *and* our heart to God. It's important to recognize that authentic prayer comes not just from the mind but also from the heart. We're not just thinking about God when we pray; we're reaching out to him with our whole being, with that deep-down part of us where we and no one else have access. Only God can totally know that part of us: our heart. The Catechism describes the heart like this:

> The heart is the dwelling-place where I am, where I live; accord-ing to the Semitic or Biblical expression, the heart is the place "to which I withdraw." The heart is our hidden center, beyond the grasp of our reason and of others; only the Spirit of God can fathom the human heart and know it fully. The heart is the place of decision, deeper than our psychic drives. It is the place of truth, where we choose life or death. It is the place of encoun-ter, because as image of God we live in relation: it is the place of covenant. (CCC 2563)

When we pray, we open our heart to God and ask him to come into it. We can only issue that invitation, however, because God is already knocking at the door of our hearts. In fact, prayer is part of how we accept God's invitation to join him, rather than the other way around. Although we were made to pray, prayer can still be difficult. It doesn't always come naturally to our fallen nature. Fortunately, God doesn't leave us to our own devices. Rather he gives us strength to persevere, and, through the words and example of Jesus, he teaches us how to pray.

During Jesus' life on earth, he demonstrated what prayer looks like through his own habits of regular prayer. One of those habits was to often retreat to a quiet and secluded place to pray (Mark 1:35, 6:46; Luke 5:16). Most of us are so busy. We hurry from one activity to the next, and even when we're alone, we fill the time with distractions—with cell phones and social media, TV, music, and videogames. By making quiet time for prayer, Jesus shows us that we need to do the same. We need to make time for him by standing up, walking away from the distractions of the world, and finding a quiet, secluded place to be with him. Even if that quiet place is just in our minds, that's still good. The important thing is tuning out the world's distractions so we can focus on him.

Jesus also taught his Apostles and disciples that prayer does not depend entirely on them. If we make the effort to find God in prayer, he will respond. He is, in fact, waiting for us: "Ask, and it will be given you; seek, and you will find; knock, and it will be opened to you. For every one who asks receives, and he who seeks finds, and to him who knocks it will be opened" (Matt 7:7–9). By this Jesus doesn't mean that we will get whatever we ask for in prayer. He means that if it is God himself for whom we're asking, if it's God, not things, whom we're seeking in prayer, then we most certainly will find him. At the same time, God still does listen to our petitions and he understand them totally. He loves us as a Father, and so he will answer our prayers in a way that is best for us and others—even when we don't understand what this might be.

> Just as Jesus prays to the Father and gives thanks before receiving his gifts, so he teaches us *filial boldness*: "Whatever you ask in prayer, believe that you receive it, and you will" [*Mk* 11:24]. Such is the power of prayer and of faith that does not doubt: "all things are possible to him who believes" [*Mk* 9:23; cf. *Mt* 21:22]. Jesus is as saddened by the "lack of faith" of his own neighbors and the "little faith" of his own disciples [Cf. *Mk* 6:6; *Mt* 8:26] as he is struck with admiration at the great faith of the Roman centurion and the Canaanite woman [Cf. *Mt* 8:10; 15:28]. (CCC 2610)

Again, prayer is a conversation with God, and it takes time, consistency, and practice to get good at it. Think of how much time you have had to spend with your best friend to gain and maintain your friendship with him or her. It's the same with God. The first time we start talking with God it might feel awkward and unfamiliar. But the more time we spend with him and the more we share our hearts with him, the more natural it will become. Before you know it, you'll pray without even thinking about it. It will feel as normal as talking to your siblings or your best friends.

All that practice really does pay off. Prayer is always worth the time and effort we put into it. It's worth persevering through the hard part. Part of perseverance, though, is humility. In prayer, we approach God himself, opening our hearts to him. In doing so, we have to realize our own lack of power in the situation and accept it. We have to take on the character of little children petitioning their father, and not let pride or our own weaknesses get in the way of going to him, opening our hearts to him, and receiving the graces he offers us.

The Lord's Prayer

One of the most important lessons about prayer that Jesus gives to us is that we must draw near to God as "*Abba/Father*." In the ancient world it was easy to view God as "Master," "King," or "Lord," and these are indeed correct titles for God. Jesus, however, changes the dynamic of our prayer by calling us to focus on God as a loving and merciful Father. We've mentioned many times already that Christians are the adopted sons and daughters of God. That's not a platitude or a nice way of speaking. It's the truth of our relationship with God, and Jesus Christ himself taught us that we should address God as "Our Father."

The audacity of calling God "Father" is expressed in the Mass. The priest leads us in the "Our Father" by saying:

At the Savior's command and formed by divine teaching, *we dare to say*: Our Father, who art in heaven . . .[1]

The "Our Father" (or "Lord's Prayer") is so familiar to us, that we may sometimes not pay much attention to the words. But this would be a mistake. Jesus himself composed this prayer and gave it to us, and in its petitions the Church has found a summary and model for all prayer. The Catechism of the Catholic Church (CCC 2759–2865) bases its teaching on prayer on the Lord's Prayer—explaining what it means to call God "Father" and how everything we should ask from God in prayer can be found in seven petitions.

---

[1] Order of Mass, in *The Roman Missal: Renewed by Decree of the Most Holy Second Ecumenical Council of the Vatican, Promulgated by Authority of Pope Paul VI and Revised at the Direction of Pope John Paul II*, third typical edition (Washington D.C.: United States Conference of Catholic Bishops, 2011), 124.

Jesus promises to intercede for us in response to our prayers: "Whatever you ask in my name, I will do it, that the Father may be glorified in the Son; if you ask anything in my name, I will do it" (John 14:13–14). Jesus is, of course, God himself, but he is also Emmanuel, God-with-us. He is accessible to us directly, and when we pray to Jesus our brother, he takes our prayers to his Father and into the very heart of the Trinity. Jesus is the great mediator between God and man. It is fitting, then, that one of the most powerful forms of prayer in the Christian tradition is the simple repetition of the name of Jesus (CCC 2665–2669).

Evangelization

Part of seeking holiness and being a disciple of Christ is sharing our faith with others. We do this through evangelization, which is the spreading of the total Christian life of discipleship and faith—essentially, the spreading of the Good News—to ever more people.

Jesus himself taught that evangelization is part of the life of discipleship, calling us to "make disciples of all nations" in Matthew 28. He also showed us what this looks like through his words and deeds. The Apostles learned from him and continued his mission after his death and Resurrection. They, in turn, entrusted the apostolic mission of evangelization to their successors, the bishops (CCC 861). But it is not just the clergy who are called to evangelize. Evangelization is a part of the general call to holiness that is shared by all the baptized.

SELECTED READING:
John Paul II, Encyclical Letter Regarding Certain Fundamental Questions of the Church's Moral Teaching *Veritatis Splendor* (August 6, 1993), nos. 6–8

The dialogue of Jesus with the rich young man, related in the nineteenth chapter of Saint Matthew's Gospel, can serve as a useful guide for listening once more in a lively and direct way to his moral teaching: "Then someone came to him and said, 'Teacher, what good must I do to have eternal life?' And he said to him, 'Why do you ask me about what is good? There is only one who is good. If you wish to enter into life, keep the commandments.' He said to him, 'Which ones?' And Jesus said, 'You shall not murder; You shall not commit adultery; You shall not steal; You shall not bear false witness; Honour your father and mother; also, You shall love your neighbour as yourself.' The young man said to him, 'I have kept all these; what do I still lack?' Jesus said to him, 'If you wish to be perfect, go, sell your possessions and give the money to the poor, and you will have treasure in heaven; then come, follow me'" (Mt 19:16–21).

"Then someone came to him. . . ." In the young man, whom Matthew's Gospel does not name, we can recognize every person who, consciously or not, approaches Christ the Redeemer of man and questions him about morality. For the young man, the question is not so much about rules to be followed, but about the full meaning of life. This is in fact the aspiration at the heart of every human decision and action, the quiet searching and interior prompting which sets freedom in motion. This question is ultimately an appeal to the absolute Good which attracts us and beckons us; it is the echo of a call from God who is the origin and goal of man's life. Precisely in this perspective the Second Vatican Council called for a renewal of moral theology, so that its teaching would display the lofty vocation which the faithful have received in Christ, the only response fully capable of satisfying the desire of the human heart.

In order to make this "encounter" with Christ possible, God willed his Church. Indeed, the Church "wishes to serve this single end: that each person may be able to find Christ, in order that Christ may walk with each person the path of life."

The question which the rich young man puts to Jesus of Nazareth is one which rises from the depths of his heart. It is an essential and unavoidable question for the life of every man, for it is about the moral good which must be done, and about eternal life. The young man senses that there is a connection between moral good and the fulfillment of his own destiny. He is a devout Israelite, raised as it were in the shadow of the Law of the Lord. If he asks Jesus this question, we can presume that it is not because he is ignorant of the answer contained in the Law. It is more likely that the attractiveness of the person of Jesus had prompted within him new questions about moral good. He feels the need to draw near to the One who had begun his preaching with this new and decisive proclamation: "The time is fulfilled, and the Kingdom of God is at hand; repent, and believe in the Gospel" (Mk 1:15).

People today need to turn to Christ once again in order to receive from him the answer to their questions about what is good and what is evil. Christ is the Teacher, the Risen One who has life in himself and who is always present in his Church and in the world. It is he who opens up to the faithful the book of the Scriptures and, by fully revealing the Father's will, teaches the truth about moral action. At the source and summit of the economy of salvation, as the Alpha and the Omega of human history (cf. Rev 1:8; 21:6; 22:13), Christ sheds light on man's condition and his integral vocation. Consequently, "the man who wishes to understand himself thoroughly— and not just in accordance with immediate, partial, often superficial, and even illusory standards and measures of his being—must with his unrest, uncertainty and even his weakness and sinfulness, with his life and death, draw near to Christ. He must, so to speak, enter him with all his own self; he must 'appropriate' and assimilate the whole of the reality of the Incarnation and Redemption in order to find himself. If this profound process takes place within him, he then bears fruit not only of adoration of God but also of deeper wonder at himself."

QUESTIONS FOR REVIEW

1. What was the purpose of the Law of Moses?
2. How does Jesus tell us we can fulfill the Law?
3. Who, in the kingdom of heaven, are the "happy" or "blessed" ones?
4. What is prayer?
5. How, at the end of time, does Jesus say each of us will be judged?

QUESTIONS FOR DISCUSSION

1. How is Jesus' understanding of happiness different from the world's? How can people who mourn or are poor in spirit be happier than those who are rich and powerful?
2. Is it easy or difficult for you to share your heart with God? Why do you think that is? What is one thing you could do every day to make more time to talk to God?
3. Have you ever shared your faith with someone? If so, did it make you uncomfortable? Why or why not?

Chapter 3

Jesus Tells Us of the Goal of This Life and of the End of Life

Assigned Reading
1 Corinthians 15:35–50
Revelation 21
CCC 1023–1029

What can we look forward to after a life dedicated to following Jesus and his teaching? Despite what cartoons might show you, it's not sitting on a bunch of puffy white clouds surrounded by angels playing harps. There is a lot of misunderstanding about life after death, which is natural, since it's a mystery—something we'll never truly be able to wrap our minds around until we experience it for ourselves . . . and maybe not even then. Even so, we can know some things based upon Sacred Scripture.

The Communion of Saints

In the Book of Revelation, St. John writes,

> After this I looked, and behold, a great multitude which no man
> could number, from every nation, from all tribes and peoples
> and tongues, standing before the throne and before the Lamb,
> clothed in white robes, with palm branches in their hands . . .
> (Rev 7:9)

In heaven, we will join all those men and women who have gone
before us and who now enjoy their reward in God's Kingdom. Even
now, though, we are united with them in the Church. The Church spans
heaven and earth, time and eternity, and in it the baptized on earth are
united with the saints in heaven. This is part of what we mean when, in
the Creed, we profess our belief in the "Communion of Saints." That
term, however, refers to more than just the saints who are already in
heaven. It also refers to the entirety of God's holy people, which includes
the Church on earth, the souls in purgatory, and the saints in heaven.
These three groups together make up the whole Church, the "Communion of Saints" (CCC 947).

Because we already experience this communion in a limited way here
on earth, we have some glimpse of what it will be like in heaven. Like
the Church on earth, the Church in heaven is a "great multitude . . . from
every nation, from all tribes and peoples and tongues" united in worship-
ping God (Rev 7:9). This means heaven will never be lonely or boring.
The blessings of human relationships—the joy that we find on earth in
love and friendship, the deep bond we form with others when we work
together on a common cause or project, even the excitement we experience in getting to know new and interesting people at a good party—will
be present and perfected in heaven.

It's also important to remember that since we are already part of this
communion, even now we are never alone in our trials, sorrows, or struggle for holiness. We have the prayers and assistance of our fellow believers on earth to support us, and (even better) the prayers of the saints in

heaven. Just as we pray for our family and friends on earth, so the saints in heaven intercede for us. We can pray to them, asking them for help in our lives, and they will take our prayers before God himself. The entire Church is united in prayer in this way. We share in each other's struggles and pray to God for each other.

> Since Abraham, intercession—asking on behalf of another—has been characteristic of a heart attuned to God's mercy. In the age of the Church, Christian intercession participates in Christ's, as an expression of the communion of saints. In intercession, he who prays looks "not only to his own interests, but also to the interests of others," even to the point of praying for those who do him harm [*Phil* 2:4; cf. *Acts* 7:60; *Lk* 23:28, 34]. (CCC 2635)

Chapter 4

The Four Last Things: Death, Judgment, Heaven, and Hell

‖ Assigned Reading
‖ Matthew 25
‖ CCC 1030–1041

Traditionally, the Church has spoken of "Four Last Things" that occur to a person as they pass from this earthly life. First we die, then we are judged, then we go to heaven (or first purgatory) or hell.

Death

While we know that we are united to the saints in heaven in the Communion of Saints, we also know that the harsh reality of death lies between us and them. Every religious tradition has tried to answer the riddle of death. Human beings in every culture have had a sense that death cannot be the end. Our seemingly infinite capacity for love and knowledge and our sense of connection to our loved ones who have gone before us in death make us believe that there must be something more for us after death. Even today, when many do claim that nothing awaits us after this life, death remains a difficult puzzle for our culture. This leads us to either hide from the reality of death, living this life as if it could go on forever, or to fight off death, asking medicine and technology to delay the inevitable. But death *is* inevitable. One day or another, everyone will die (CCC 1006).

As Christians, we know by faith that human beings weren't created by God to die and disappear. We're not just material beings. Unlike vacuum cleaners, computers, and badly-cared-for house plants, we don't cease to exist when our body stops working. This truth is beautifully presented to us in the Book of Genesis. In Genesis 2, which recounts the story of man's creation, the Bible tells us that God formed man out of the dust of the earth and breathed into his nostrils the breath of life (Gen 2:7). This teaches us that each human being is composed of a material body and a spiritual soul, which doesn't decompose and die like a material body. Later in Genesis, we learn that even bodily death was contrary to God's original plan for us. Death wasn't supposed to be a part of our existence. Rather, it's a consequence of sin (Gen 2:17, 3:3, 3:19; Wis 2:23–24). This is why death—which is, in a way, a completely natural part of all bodily life—is a problem and riddle for us. We sense that there is more to us than what returns to the earth when we die and that there is something "wrong" about death (CCC 1006–1008).

Jesus provides us with the answer to the riddle of death. He says, "I am the resurrection and the life; he who believes in me, though he die, yet shall he live, and whoever lives and believes in me shall never die" (John 11:25–26). Through his life, death and resurrection, Jesus defeated sin and death. If we unite ourselves to him, we will die in the sense that our earthly life will end, but we will, in fact, live forever with him. This means that, for the Christian, death is transformed by Christ from a curse to a blessing—it becomes the gateway to eternal life (CCC 1009). "Christ is Risen from the dead. By death He trampled death, and to those in the tombs He granted life!"[1]

---

[1]   Eastern Orthodox Church, "Paschal Troparion," The Divine Liturgy of St. John Chrysostom of the Eastern Orthodox Church, ed. George Mastrantonis (New York: Greek Orthodox Archdiocese of North and South America, 1966).

Judgment

After our death we first will be called to give an account of our actions before God. There will be nowhere to hide. There will be no excuses or rationalizations. God sees our hearts and knows us better than we know ourselves. Christ will be our judge:

> Christ is Lord of eternal life. Full right to pass definitive judgment on the works and hearts of men belongs to him as redeemer of the world. He "acquired" this right by his cross. The Father has given "all judgment to the Son" [*Jn* 5:22; cf. 5:27; *Mt* 25:31; *Acts* 10:42; 17:31; *2 Tim* 4:1]. Yet the Son did not come to judge, but to save and to give the life he has in himself [Cf. *Lk* 21:12; *Jn* 15:19–20]. By rejecting grace in this life, one already judges oneself, receives according to one's works, and can even condemn oneself for all eternity by rejecting the Spirit of love [Cf. *Jn* 3:18; 12:48; *Mt* 12:32; *1 Cor* 3:12–15; *Heb* 6:4–6; 10:26–31]. (CCC 679)

This particular judgment occurs at the moment of our death. When we die, each of us will be judged according to our works and our acceptance or refusal of grace. Each of us will either enter heaven immediately, enter hell immediately, or have to be purified in purgatory before entering heaven (CCC 1022).

The general (or last) judgment will occur at the end of time when the dead rise from their graves and Jesus returns in glory. At that time, our souls will be reunited with our bodies, and the just will experience the resurrection of life—they will be like the risen Christ—but the unjust will go forth to the "resurrection of judgment" (John 5:28–29). The fate of each individual is determined at the particular judgment he or she experiences immediately after death, but at the last judgment, God will reveal all things. He will make known the full truth of our actions, our relationship with him, and his work of creation and salvation (CCC 1038–1041).

The reality of judgment shouldn't make us lose hope, but should instead urge us to conversion. It is Jesus himself who will judge us, and this is our reason for hope, because we know that his mission is to save (John 3:17). In Jesus Christ, God offers us forgiveness, grace, and friendship, but we must accept this offer of grace and friendship now, in this life. We must be ready, for we do not know the hour when we will face death and judgment (Matt 25:13).

Heaven

Purgatory

Sin not only requires forgiveness, but also satisfaction. For example, if you break your neighbor's window, not only do you need to ask for forgiveness, but you also need to pay for a replacement. This is the reason why the priest gives us a penance to do after we go to Confession. If a faithful person reaches the end of life and dies in the friendship of God but has not yet made full satisfaction for his sins, the mercy of God embraces him in purgatory.

Purgatory is a place of purification where God prepares us for the glory of heaven. The souls in purgatory suffer greatly, but they also know that they will ultimately enjoy beatitude, and so their suffering is infused with a kind of joy. Our prayers can help them in their progress toward heaven, so the Church has always urged us to pray for the dead, undertake works of penance, and offer the sacrifice of the Mass on their behalf (CCC 1032).

Heaven

If you had to describe heaven with one word, it would be "joy." This is because in heaven, you are with the source of all joy. Popular pictures of heaven always fall short of depicting this. Many can even distort our image of joy, confusing us about it or preventing us from seeing the true peace, happiness, beauty, and love that awaits us there. 1 Corinthians 2:9

calls what awaits us in heaven, "What no eye has seen, nor ear heard, nor the heart of man conceived, what God has prepared for those who love him." This helps us remember that our analogies and ideas about our eternal lives in the presence of God can't help but fall short. We can't imagine what it will be like to be in the very presence of the Trinity. We can only anticipate the great surprise that heaven will be.

Perhaps most importantly, popular conceptions of heaven leave out the fact that, as the theologian N.T. Wright often says, "heaven is important but it's not the end of the world." As we learned above, God created us as both body and soul, and death was not his original plan for us. We are not really complete without our bodies, and so the final act of God's plan is the resurrection of the dead.

In the resurrection, all people will rise from the dead, our souls will be reunited with our bodies, and the just will take their place co-ruling with Christ over a new creation (see Wis 3:1–9). This marvelous message of hope for creation is often overlooked and forgotten, but in reality it is the most thrilling doctrine of Christian eschatology. God bringing about the marriage of heaven and earth in the New Creation (see Rev 21:1–5) is a marvelously hopeful and exciting finale to the plan of salvation. Jesus saves not only souls, but bodies, and all of creation! And (hopefully) each of us will get to enjoy that salvific act for all eternity in a physical heaven!

Hell

Many people don't believe in hell because they can't see how a good God could ever send someone to such a place. They are right that God would never send someone to hell. They are wrong, however, that this means no one goes to hell. The truth is that God does not send anyone to hell. If you are a friend of God in life, you are a friend of God in death. But, if you are not a friend of God in life, you aren't forced to be a friend of God in death. God respects our freedom, and if you have chosen to be separated from God, if you have chosen not to love him and not to enter into a relationship with him, hell is the eternal place where you can continue this separation from God.

Hell is an unfortunate reality that teaches us about the justice of God and his gift of free will. Heaven is a communion of love, and love, by its very nature, is given freely. God loves us. If we love him back, we can go to heaven. If we do not return his love, we will experience existence without God. And an eternity without God is hell. Of course, God desires all to be saved: "This is good, and it is acceptable in the sight of God our Savior, who desires all men to be saved and to come to the knowledge of the truth" (1 Tim 2:3–4) and Christ died, ". . . once for all, the righteous for the unrighteous, that he might bring us to God" (1 Pet 3:18), but salvation is a gift freely given, and we are just as free to reject it.

SELECTED READING:
Pope Benedict XVI, Encyclical Letter on Christian Hope
Spe Salvi (November 30, 2007), nos. 44–47

To protest against God in the name of justice is not helpful. A world without God is a world without hope (cf. Eph 2:12). Only God can create justice. And faith gives us the certainty that he does so. The image of the Last Judgement is not primarily an image of terror, but an image of hope; for us it may even be the decisive image of hope. Is it not also a frightening image? I would say: it is an image that evokes responsibility, an image, therefore, of that fear of which Saint Hilary spoke when he said that all our fear has its place in love. God is justice and creates justice. This is our consolation and our hope. And in his justice there is also grace. This we know by turning our gaze to the crucified and risen Christ. Both these things—justice and grace—must be seen in their correct inner relationship. Grace does not cancel out justice. It does not make wrong into right. It is not a sponge which wipes everything away, so that whatever someone has done on earth ends up being of equal value. Dostoevsky, for example, was right to protest against this kind of Heaven and this kind of grace in his novel *The Brothers Karamazov*. Evildoers, in the end, do not sit at table at the eternal banquet beside their victims without distinction, as though nothing had happened. Here I would like to quote a passage from Plato which expresses a premonition of just judgment that in many respects remains true and salutary for Christians too. Albeit using mythological images, he expresses the truth with an unambiguous clarity, saying that in the end souls will stand naked before the judge. It no longer matters what they once were in history, but only what they are in truth: "Often, when it is the king or some other monarch or potentate that he (the judge) has to deal with, he finds that there is no soundness in the soul whatever; he finds it scourged and scarred by the various acts of perjury and wrong-doing . . . ; it is twisted and warped by lies and vanity, and nothing is straight because truth has had no part in its development. Power, luxury, pride, and debauchery have left it so full of disproportion and ugliness that when he has inspected it (he) sends it straight to prison, where on its arrival it will undergo the appropriate punishment . . . Sometimes, though, the eye of the judge lights on a different soul which has lived in purity and truth . . . then he is struck with admiration and sends him to the isles of the blessed." In the parable of the rich man and Lazarus (cf. Lk 16:19–31), Jesus admonishes us through the image of a soul destroyed by arrogance and opulence, who has created an impassable chasm between himself and the poor man; the chasm of being trapped within material pleasures; the chasm of forgetting the other, of incapacity to love, which then becomes a burning and unquenchable thirst. We must note that in this parable Jesus is not referring to the final destiny after the Last Judgement, but is taking up a notion found, inter alia, in early Judaism, namely that of an intermediate state between death and resurrection, a state in which the final sentence is yet to be pronounced.

This early Jewish idea of an intermediate state includes the view that these souls are not simply in a sort of temporary custody but, as the parable of the rich man illustrates, are already being punished or are experiencing a provisional form of bliss. There is also the idea that this state can involve purification and healing which mature the soul for communion with God. The early Church took up these concepts, and in the Western Church they gradually developed into the doctrine of Purgatory. We do not need to examine here the complex historical paths of this development; it is enough to ask what it actually means. With death, our life-choice becomes definitive—our life stands before the judge. Our choice, which in the course of an entire life takes on a certain shape, can have a variety of forms. There can be people who have totally destroyed their desire for truth and readiness to love, people for whom everything has become a lie, people who have lived for hatred and have suppressed all love within themselves. This is a terrifying thought, but alarming profiles of this type can be seen in certain figures of our own history. In such people all would be beyond remedy and the destruction of good would be irrevocable: this is what we mean by the word *Hell*. On the other hand there can be people who are utterly pure, completely permeated by God, and thus fully open to their neighbours—people for whom communion with God even now gives direction to their entire being and whose journey towards God only brings to fulfilment what they already are.

Yet we know from experience that neither case is normal in human life. For the great majority of people—we may suppose—there remains in the depths of their being an ultimate interior openness to truth, to love, to God. In the concrete choices of life, however, it is covered over by ever new compromises with evil—much filth covers purity, but the thirst for purity remains and it still constantly re-emerges from all that is base and remains present in the soul. What happens to such individuals when they appear before the Judge? Will all the impurity they have amassed through life suddenly cease to matter? What else might occur? Saint Paul, in his *First Letter to the Corinthians*, gives us an idea of the differing impact of God's judgement according to each person's particular circumstances. He does this using images which in some way try to express the invisible, without it being possible for us to conceptualize these images—simply because we can neither see into the world beyond death nor do we have any experience of it. Paul begins by saying that Christian life is built upon a common foundation: Jesus Christ. This foundation endures. If we have stood firm on this foundation and built our life upon it, we know that it cannot be taken away from us even in death. Then Paul continues: "Now if any one builds on the foundation with gold, silver, precious stones, wood, hay, straw—each man's work will become manifest; for the Day will disclose it, because it will be revealed with fire, and the fire will test what sort of work each one has done. If the work which any man has built on the foundation survives, he will receive a reward. If any man's work is burned up, he will suffer loss, though he himself will be saved, but only as through fire" (1 Cor 3:12–15). In this text, it is in any case evident that our salvation can take different forms, that some of what is built may be burned down, that in order to be saved we personally have to pass through "fire" so as to become fully open to receiving God and able to take our place at the table of the eternal marriage-feast.

Some recent theologians are of the opinion that the fire which both burns and saves is Christ himself, the Judge and Saviour. The encounter with him is the decisive act of judgement. Before his gaze all falsehood melts away. This encounter with him, as it burns us, transforms and frees us, allowing us to become truly ourselves. All that we build during our lives can prove to be mere straw, pure bluster, and it collapses. Yet in the pain of this encounter, when the impurity and sickness of our lives become evident to us, there lies salvation. His gaze, the touch of his heart heals us through an undeniably painful transformation "as through fire." But it is a blessed pain, in which the holy power of his love sears through us like a flame, enabling us to become totally ourselves and thus totally of God. In this way the inter-relation between justice and grace also becomes clear: the way we live our lives is not immaterial, but our defilement does not stain us for ever if we have at least continued to reach out towards Christ, towards truth and towards love. Indeed, it has already been burned away through Christ's Passion. At the moment of judgement we experience and we absorb the overwhelming power of his love over all the evil in the world and in ourselves. The pain of love becomes our salvation and our joy. It is clear that we cannot calculate the "duration" of this transforming burning in terms of the chronological measurements of this world. The transforming "moment" of this encounter eludes earthly time-reckoning—it is the heart's time, it is the time of "passage" to communion with God in the Body of Christ. The judgement of God is hope, both because it is justice and because it is grace. If it were merely grace, making all earthly things cease to matter, God would still owe us an answer to the question about justice—the crucial question that we ask of history and of God. If it were merely justice, in the end it could bring only fear to us all. The incarnation of God in Christ has so closely linked the two together—judgement and grace—that justice is firmly established: we all work out our salvation "with fear and trembling" (Phil 2:12). Nevertheless grace allows us all to hope, and to go trustfully to meet the Judge whom we know as our "advocate," or *parakletos* (cf. 1 Jn 2:1).

QUESTIONS FOR REVIEW

1. What three groups make up the Church?
2. How can the saints help those of us on earth?
3. What are the Four Last Things?
4. What two types of judgment will we face?
5. Who ultimately decides who goes to heaven and who goes to hell?

QUESTIONS FOR DISCUSSION

1. Does it make you uncomfortable to think or talk about death? Why or why not?
2. Why do you think anyone would choose to go to hell?
3. Knowing that God knows all, and that at the last judgment, every good act and every bad act you've ever done will be made known to all, can you think of one thing in your life you'd like to start or stop doing?

This reflection on our human freedom leads us to the final part of this course: tackling some challenges that we will face in the world because of our faith in Christ.

Appendix

CHALLENGES

How Can We Know God Really Exists?

It is often thought that belief in God is simply a matter of blind faith, with "faith" defined as "believing something without evidence" (or, even, "believing something in spite of the evidence"). People are often surprised to learn that the Catholic Church directly rejects this view.

At the First Vatican Council (1869–1870), the Church affirmed that "God . . . can be known with certainty from the created world by the natural light of human reason [Vatican Council I, *Dei Filius* 2: DS 3004; cf. 3026; Vatican Council II, *Dei Verbum* 6]" (CCC 36).

In other words, even without the Bible or Tradition or the teaching of the Church, that is, without divine Revelation, a person can know that God exists. As we saw earlier, there are two primary ways of coming to this knowledge: reflecting on the physical world around us and reflecting on our experience as human persons.

There are many different arguments that can be developed by looking at the physical world around us. We will consider two. First, the argument from the contingency of the world. The word "contingent" means that something is dependent on something else for its existence; or, put another way, it doesn't explain its own existence. Something that is contingent does not have to exist. Now, our whole universe (and every part of it) is contingent. It is here, it exists, but it does not have to exist. So the question naturally arises: If the universe doesn't need to be here, why is it here?

The existence of a contingent thing, then, points to something else beyond itself. If a thing does not explain the reason for its own existence, we have to look for something else that does explain its existence. This search ultimately leads us to something that, so to speak, *possesses* existence; it does not receive existence from another; it is something, in other words, that is *not* contingent. This ultimate reality, which exists in itself, is God: the fullness of existence.

A second argument for God's existence from looking at the physical world is based on the intelligibility of the world. To say that the world is *intelligible* means that it can be understood. Think of the natural sciences (like biology, chemistry, and physics). When we study the world around us, we find something amazing: we can understand it! We can discover different laws that govern the way that different parts of the universe work together and relate to one another. So, for example, we are able to recognize and explain the way that photosynthesis occurs, why particular atoms combine to form molecules, and why objects in motion tend to stay in motion unless acted upon. Our minds are able to recognize and develop equations for the things that we see happening around us. But that should cause us to ask a question: Where does this intelligibility come from? Why, when we look around us, do we discover all of this order in the universe?

Ultimately, the order of the universe points us to an intelligent Creator of all things. Our minds can understand the world around us because the world itself comes forth from a mind—the mind of God. In a very real way, when we study the world through the different sciences, our mind comes into an encounter with the mind of God. It is interesting that many scientists (even some who are not Christians) have spoken this way when discussing their work. Albert Einstein famously said: "I want to know God's thoughts—the rest are mere details."

This argument is particularly important since science is often viewed as opposed to faith. What is so interesting is that, rather than proving the non-existence of God, science itself actually points us toward an intelligent Creator of the universe.

In addition to these arguments from the physical world around us, we can also look at the experience of the human person as another way of recognizing God's existence. Again, there are two main ways that we can approach this.

The first is by way of the natural law. All of us, as human beings, have an innate sense of right and wrong, good and evil. It has become popular in our day to say that all morality is relative. This is the belief that there is no such thing as what is "right and wrong for everyone," but only what *you think* is right and wrong and what *I think* is right and wrong. We often hear people say: "That may be right in your view, but it's wrong in my view."

But, ultimately, no one actually believes this deep down. Even young children recognize when a situation is "not fair." Notice, the child is not merely saying "I don't like that." Rather, the child appeals to an objective standard of "fairness" and "justice" and is pointing out that this particular situation does not measure up to that standard. The ultimate standard of goodness, against which we measure all moral actions, is God himself, who is perfect goodness.

A second pointer to God rooted in our experience as human beings is the longing for God that we find within our hearts. In the Catechism we read: "The desire for God is written in the human heart, because man is created by God and for God; and God never ceases to draw man to himself. Only in God will he find the truth and happiness he never stops searching for" (CCC 27). One common experience that we all share is this experience of being unsatisfied, restless, and unfulfilled. Even when things are going well in our lives, we still recognize that things could be more perfect, more complete.

We search for meaning, for truth, for happiness; and, when we can't find it, we often experience anxiety and discouragement. This desire points us to a higher reality. It reminds us that we are made for something greater than this world. That is why this world always fails to fully satisfy us. We are made for God. God is infinite truth, infinite goodness, infinite beauty, and infinite love; it is only in God that our desire will come to rest. "You have made us for yourself, O Lord, and our hearts are restless until they rest in you."[1]

So, we can come to knowledge of God's existence through the use of our natural reason (our mind), by looking at the physical world around us and our own experience. But we can also go beyond this through faith. Faith, we should recall, is a form of knowledge.

Let's put the question of God aside for a minute. We use a type of faith all the time in our day-to-day lives, whenever we believe something on the word of another. Think of a couple of examples. We place our faith in our parents when they tell us the date of our birthday. We were not conscious of what happened on the day of our birth (or for the first few years of our lives). We take our parents' word for it when they tell us about our earliest days. Likewise, at school, we take the word of the athletic director when he makes an announcement that a game is cancelled or rescheduled. Most of us don't go to the field "just to check." Many times a day, we take the word of a trustworthy source. Now, God is the ultimate trustworthy source. Whereas human beings can make mistakes or lie to us, God is all knowing and all good, so he never makes mistakes and never deceives. Therefore, his Word is totally reliable, and it is perfectly reasonable to believe what he tells us.

Let's take this a step further. Beyond just believing what another person tells us, this everyday faith also plays a critical role in our relationships. The only way to really come into a deep relationship with another person is through faith. We believe what this person tells us about themselves and about how they feel about us. We have no access to the inner world and inner life of another human being unless they open that up to us and share it with us. Often, over time, as we grow to know a person better, faith goes a step further. We don't merely believe what the other person tells us, but we trust the person, we believe *in* him or her.

If this is true of other human persons, how much more so with God. His word is absolutely trustworthy, since he is omniscient and omnibenevolent. The only way to come to know the mystery of God's inner

---

[1] Augustine of Hippo, *Confessions*, bk. 1, chap. 1.

world and inner life is if he reveals himself to us. And God has revealed himself fully through the person of Jesus Christ. He has become one of us. He has entered our world as a man and given us access to his own divine life (this is what we mean by "grace").

Many people have testified to this reality. We have, of course, the testimony of the witnesses from Scripture, in both the Old and New Testaments. We also have the experiences of the saints, who have known God in this deeply personal way. Additionally, we have the faith of those we know personally: members of our family, friends, teachers, and priests.

Finally, we can have a personal experience of faith in God. Earlier, we saw that faith is a "gift of God." In other words, we can come to have the experience of receiving this gift, the experience of God raising our minds beyond their natural powers in order to come to a more personal knowledge of him. How do we grow in this way? Through prayer and the sacraments. We ask God to give us a deeper faith, to help us to know him ever more fully.

In concluding this section, it is important to see that reason and faith are in no way in conflict with one another, but are complementary in leading us to deeper knowledge of God.

There Are Some Who See Human Suffering and Conclude That God Does Not Care about Us (or That He Does Not Exist). Why Do We Say That God Loves Us Deeply?

One of the greatest obstacles to faith in God is the experience of suffering. It can be challenging to believe that God loves and cares for us given what we suffer. To begin, we will look at reasons for believing that God loves us; in the next section, we will consider why God allows evil and suffering to exist at all.

God reveals his love for us in many ways. The first is in the act of creation. God creates us freely out of love. But what does this mean? "[Creation] proceeds from God's free will; he wanted to make his creatures share in his being, wisdom and goodness" (CCC 295). To love another means to will what is good for the other. God wills that we share in his own goodness. Love also desires union with the one who is loved. It is important to see that God does not only give us good things, he gives us his very self, desiring "intimate communion" with us (CCC 54).

All of God's visible creation shares in his goodness, but human beings do so in a unique way. The first chapter of the book of Genesis affirms:

> Then God said, "Let us make man in our image, after our likeness . . . So God created man in his own image, in the image of God he created him; male and female he created them." (Gen 1:26–27)

To bear the image of God indicates that we possess reason and free will, that is, we are capable of knowledge and love. As a consequence, human beings possess a special dignity:

> Of all visible creatures only man is "able to know and love his creator" [GS 12 § 3]. He is "the only creature on earth that God has willed for its own sake" [GS 24 § 3], and he alone is called to share, by knowledge and love, in God's own life. It was for this end that he was created, and this is the fundamental reason for his dignity. (CCC 356)

God wishes to make us "partakers of the divine nature" (2 Pet 1:4). We have the capacity to give and to receive love and, in this way, we are most like God himself, who is a loving communion of three Persons: Father, Son, and Holy Spirit.

God's love is further revealed in the person of Jesus Christ. If we are capable of giving and receiving love, we are also capable of choosing not to love, and refusing the love that is offered us. This is what we mean by sin. Sin is a refusal to love God and others, and a refusal to receive their love. But even when we choose to live in this way, God does not abandon us. Rather, he enters into the brokenness and suffering of our world to bring us back to himself. Since our disobedience separated us from the life of God, Jesus came and lived a life of perfect obedience, even unto death. He died for us so that we could be restored to his friendship and attain the communion with him for which we were created.

Jesus works here and now to make this a reality in each of our lives, in a particular way through the sacraments of the Church: "By the action of Christ and the power of the Holy Spirit [the Sacraments] make present efficaciously the grace they signify" (CCC 1084). The Sacraments communicate grace to us, and the Catechism emphasizes that grace "is a *participation in the life of God*" (CCC 1997).

Through Baptism, we receive the Holy Spirit: "The desire and work of the Spirit in the heart of the Church is that we may live from the life of the risen Christ" (CCC 1091). The Holy Spirit is constantly at work to bring us to holiness: "The Holy Spirit, whom Christ the head pours out on his members, builds, animates, and sanctifies the Church" (CCC 747).

Furthermore, this is not merely an abstract reality: God's love can be experienced in a direct and personal way each day of our lives. Divine providence refers to God's guidance of creation and his constant care for all creatures: "divine providence is concrete and immediate; God cares for all, from the least things to the great events of the world and its history" (CCC 303). God reveals himself through the persons and events of our lives. Through prayer, we can come to an ever greater appreciation of God's closeness and recognize the signs of his love each day.

Divine Revelation, transmitted by the Church through Scripture and Tradition, makes God's plan of love clear to us. The story of salvation history, recorded in the pages of Scripture, is a testimony to this love. The Church actively proclaims these truths of Scripture in the liturgy and through her teachings. The Church, established by Christ, is a living voice that continues to proclaim God's love generation after generation.

How Can People Say That God Is Good If Evil and Suffering Are Present in the World?

In the preceding section, we saw ample evidence of God's love for us. He creates us in a sheer act of love, desires eternal communion with us, and, even when we turn from him, he does not abandon us in our sin, but continues working to restore us to himself, even becoming man and dying for our sake.

But why does God allow suffering and evil to be present in the world at all? How can we say that God is good when there is so much evil?

We begin by affirming that God is infinitely good and that, therefore, everything he creates is good. In several places in the creation account of Genesis 1, we see the refrain "God saw that it was good." Evil, as a consequence, is not created by God; he is not the cause of it. Suffering and evil come into the world through sin.

In the beginning, when God created the first human beings, they were not subject to suffering or death. As we saw above, however, human beings are truly free. We are capable of making decisions, of choosing to love or not to love, of responding to God's love for us or refusing him. We were given a unique place in creation. We were called to show forth God's goodness to his creation, and also to offer all of creation back to God. We were the hinge between the material world and its Creator. In rejecting God, our first parents opened the way for suffering and evil to enter the world. To understand why human sin can have such an impact on the world around us, consider an image from Peter Kreeft:

> To help understand creation and the Fall, the image of three iron rings suspended from a magnet is helpful. The magnet symbolizes God; the first ring, the soul; the middle ring, the body; and the bottom ring, nature. As long as the soul stays in touch with God, the magnetic life keeps flowing through the whole chain, from divine life to soul life, body life and nature life. The three rings stay harmonized, united, magnetized. But when the soul freely declares its independence from God [through sin], when the first iron ring separates from the magnet, the inevitable consequence is that the whole chain of rings is demagnetized and falls apart.[2]

---

[2] Peter Kreeft and Ronald Tacelli, SJ, *Handbook of Catholic Apologetics* (San Francisco: Ignatius, 2009), 143.

We live in the aftermath of this event. God did not create this situation, though he does allow it. But why? Why doesn't God just destroy all evil and suffering? The problem here comes back to free will. God created human beings (and angels) as free creatures. While this freedom is intended for good and for love, it can also be used to turn away from love, goodness, and God. When human beings choose sin, God allows them to make the choice and to experience the genuine consequences of that choice. If God did not allow us to make evil choices and to experience the consequences of those choices, it's hard to see how we could actually be free. We would merely be puppets whose actions were predetermined by God.

So God does not create evil and suffering, but he does permit them. However, God does not stop there. He actively works to bring good out of evil. Sometimes we can see this in our life, when something evil ends up leading to a greater good; other times, we will only know in the next life: "Faith gives us the certainty that God would not permit an evil if he did not cause a good to come from that very evil, by ways that we shall fully know only in eternal life" (CCC 324).

Furthermore, God does not do this "from a distance." Rather, he enters our world as a man, and takes upon himself the realities of suffering and death. In the horror of the Passion, "the sacrifice of Christ secretly becomes the source from which the forgiveness of our sins will pour forth inexhaustibly" (CCC 1851). So even in the midst of suffering and pain, even in death, our Lord is not far from us. Only sin can separate us from God; if we are in union with Christ, we can trust that he can bring good out of our suffering and even our death, for "[f]rom the greatest moral evil ever committed—the rejection and murder of God's only Son, caused by the sins of all men—God, by his grace that 'abounded all the more' [Cf. *Rom* 5:20], brought the greatest of goods: the glorification of Christ and our redemption" (CCC 312). In union with Christ we participate in his suffering, and our own suffering plays a role in the redemption of the world.

Evil is a great mystery. Facing evil in our lives and in the world around us requires great faith in God. In Scripture, we can find consolation and hope in the insights of the Psalms, Job, the prophets, and especially in the hope that comes through the Resurrection of Christ, his great victory over suffering and death. Also, approaching this issue intellectually will only take us so far; this is something that we must bring to, and wrestle with, in prayer.

Does God Really Want Us to Be Happy?

Since God created us out of love, we can be sure that he desires our happiness. We are not fulfilling a need for God or providing him with something he lacks. Thus, we can always trust that he has our ultimate good in mind.

Since God created us for himself, our happiness lies in him; unhappiness results from sin, our turning from God. But even when we had chosen to turn away from him, God sent his Son to lead us back to the way of happiness.

Jesus explicitly affirms his desire for our happiness: "These things I have spoken to you, that my joy may be in you, and that your joy may be full" (John 15:11). At the heart of Jesus' teaching stand the Beatitudes ("Blessed are..."). The Greek word *makarios*, which is translated as "blessed," could also be translated as "happy." The way of the beatitudes is the way to true happiness.

Saint Paul further affirms this view by recognizing joy as a mark of a true Christian, identifying it as one of the fruits of the Holy Spirit (see Gal 5:22). Christians are called to "Rejoice always in the Lord" (Phil 4:4). Even in the midst of suffering, we are called to retain this spirit of happiness and joy, placing our hope in the Risen Christ who has conquered suffering and death and will bring his faithful to the everlasting joy of heaven.

Isn't It True That the Catholic Church Invented the Dogmas and Doctrines That It Professes? Since These Are Man-Made Teachings, We Don't Have to Believe Them, and We Should Distrust the Church.

The content of this question can help us to understand why Jesus established a Church in the first place. Put yourself in his position. The Son of God has lowered himself to take on human nature, going even to the shameful death of the Cross to save us from sin. He then rises from the dead, revealing his victory over sin and death. Is it likely that he would then simply ascend back into heaven and hope that his life and message would be spread to all people? No. Rather, he would establish an institution whose mission was to bring the message of salvation to the world. Something this important would not be left to chance.

Given this fact, the Church is not merely a club or fan group which arose in the aftermath of the Resurrection. If this were the case, the Church would be merely a human organization. But the New Testament tells us that Jesus himself established the Church—it is *his* Church. Furthermore, the true Church of Christ is the one founded on St. Peter: "And I tell you, you are Peter, and on this rock I will build my Church, and the powers of death shall not prevail against it" (Matt 16:18).

"I will build *my* Church." The Catholic Church today, nearly 2000 years later, continues the line of St. Peter in the papacy. Pope Francis is the 266th pope of the Catholic Church. A quick online search will give you the entire list with names and the dates that they served as pope. Jesus promised Peter that the "powers of death" would never prevail against the Church. Before ascending into heaven, Jesus assured his followers, "I am with you always, to the close of the age" (Matt 28:20).

One way that this presence reveals itself is in the gift of infallibility, which Jesus has entrusted to the Church: "In order to preserve the Church in the purity of the faith handed on by the apostles, Christ who is the Truth willed to confer on her a share in his own infallibility" (CCC 889). In her official teachings on matters of faith and morals, the Church is preserved from all error; thus we can be assured that the genuine teaching of Jesus is communicated to us through the Church.

APPENDIX

How Do Catholics Answer Questions about the Blessed Virgin Mary?

The Catholic Church has a rich tradition of devotion to the Blessed Virgin Mary, but this devotion is often misunderstood. First, it is important to note that Catholics do not worship Mary. Worship and adoration are given to God alone. To the saints, we offer veneration and honor. The tradition has three terms that help us make these distinctions: *latria, dulia,* and *hyperdulia. Latria* is a Latin word used to refer to the adoration due to God alone; *dulia* is a Greek word which refers to the veneration or honor given to the saints. Because of Mary's unique relationship with Jesus, a special term, *hyperdulia,* is used to describe the "super"-honor given to her by the faithful. Mary is a creature, so she does not receive the adoration that is given to God alone. At the same time, she is the greatest of creatures, the greatest of all the saints. And so, we offer this special veneration to her. It is worth noting that we follow our Lord's example in doing this. We are certain that Jesus perfectly lived the commandments of God, including the command to "Honor your father and your mother" (Exod 20:12). Like Jesus, we too honor Mary, whom Jesus gave us to be our mother as well (see John 19:26–27).

When we pray to Mary, we are asking her to intercede for us with God. All grace finds its source in God alone; but in his wisdom and goodness, he has willed to communicate grace to us through Mary (and the other saints). Since Mary is in heaven, in the direct presence of the Lord, she knows better than we do what is truly for our good. If we ask our friends and family to pray for us here on earth, how much more should we ask for the prayers of those who are in the direct presence of God in heaven?! Certainly we can (and should) pray to God directly. But, insofar as God calls us as a community of believers, as a Church, he wills that his saints (and Mary in a particular way) be instrumental in communicating his graces throughout his Church.

Another area of confusion in regard to Mary is the reference in the Gospels to the "brothers and sisters" of Jesus (see Matt 13:53–58). Catholics affirm the "perpetual virginity" of Mary, and so believe that

164

Jesus is the only Son of Mary. So what are we to make of these words in the Gospels?

There are several ways we can approach this. First, it is important to note that the word used for brother can also be used to refer to extended family, like cousins. Let's look carefully at Matthew's Gospel. In Matthew 13, two of the "brothers" of Jesus that are mentioned are James and Joseph. But, later in the Gospel, Matthew speaks of the "other Mary" (Matt 27:61) who was present at the Crucifixion of Jesus, and identifies her specifically as "the mother of James and Joseph" (Matt 27:56). This "other Mary" is further identified in the Gospel of John: "But standing by the cross of Jesus were his mother, and his mother's sister, Mary the wife of Clopas, and Mary Magdalene" (John 19:25). It appears that "Mary the wife of Clopas" is the "other Mary" mentioned in Matthew's Gospel. Amazingly, Eusebius of Caesarea, and early Church historian, makes reference to Clopas and identifies his sons as cousins of Jesus.

There is also other evidence in the Scriptures to support the view that Jesus is the only child of Mary. Think back to the Annunciation. When the Angel Gabriel tells Mary that she will bear a child she responds by saying "How can this be?"